PRAYERS FOR MERCY

CRYING FOR GOD'S MERCY, GOD'S
MERCY IS INEXHAUSTIBLE

PRAYER M. MADUEKE

ISBN: 978-1658537506

Published by **Prayer Publications**

259 Wainwright Street, Newark,

New Jersey 07112 United States.

From The Author

Prayer M. Madueke
CHRISTIAN AUTHOR

My name is Prayer Madueke. I'm a spiritual warrior in the lord's vineyard. An accomplished author, speaker and expert on spiritual warfare and deliverance. I've published well over 100 books on every area of successful Christian living. I'm an acclaimed family and relationship counselor with several of titles dealing with those critical areas in the lives of the children of God. I travel to several countries each year speaking and conducting deliverance, breaking the yokes of demonic oppression and setting captives free.

I will be delighted to partner with you also in organized crusades, ceremonies, marriages and marriage seminars, special events, church ministration and fellowship for the advancement of God's kingdom here on earth.

All my books can be found Amazon.com. Visit my website www.madueke.com for powerful devotionals and materials.

Free Book Gift

Just to say Thank You for getting my book: Prayers For

Mercy, I'll like to give you these books for free:

The link to download them are at the end of this book.

Your testimonies will abound. Click here to see my other books. They have produced many testimonies and I want your testimony to be one too.

Prayer Requests or Counselling

Send me an email on prayermadu@yahoo.com if you need prayers or counsel or you have questions. Better still if you want to be friends with me.

TABLE OF CONTENTS

1. What Is God's Mercy? 9

2. Who Needs God's Mercy? 16

3. The Power Of God's Mercy............................43

4. The Position Of God's Mercy 67

5. Purpose Of God's Mercy................................92

6. Benefits Of God's Mercy - 1 118

7. Benefits Of God's Mercy - 2 180

8. How To Receive Mercy 185

9. 3 Days Decree For Mercy............................202

WARFARE SECTION

• Mercy Of God To Turn Away God's Anger..............228

• Mercy Of God, Destroy Judgment Against Me 232

• Mercy To Reverse Evil Consequences.....................235

- Mercy Of God, Blot Out My Transgression 238

- Mercy To Return God Back To Me 241

- Mercy Of God, Destroy My Sins................................244

- Justification By Divine Mercy.....................................247

- Mercy Of God, Empower Me To Walk With God 251

- Mercy Of God, Remove Me From Oppression..........254

- Mercy Of God, Deliver Me From Suffering...............257

- Mercy Of God, Deliver Me From Evil Wasters 261

- Mercy Of God, Position Me To Fight 264

- Mercy Of God, Fight For Me 267

- Mercy Of God, Vindicate Me.....................................270

- Mercy Of God, Hear My Prayers...............................273

- Mercy Of God, Remember Me 276

- Mercy Of God, See Me Through................................279

Chapter 1

WHAT IS GOD'S MERCY?

When God anointed Jesus Christ of Nazareth with the Holy Ghost and with power, the mercy of God accompanied the anointing. The result was that he went about doing good. His ministry of mercy was healing all that were possessed of the devil. The mercy of God is for all; however, it cannot be forced on anyone without his choice. No matter your religion, you are qualified to obtain mercy from

God if you demand it through faith, obedience to God, and not through disobedience and false hope.

Mercy can be translated as kindness, loving kindness, good, goodness, pity, and compassion. It is a deep and tender feeling of compassion. God's mercy entails His having a deep and tender feeling of compassion towards us. It is actually being compassionate and aroused by the sight of weakness or suffering. It means to bend or stoop in kindness or loyalty to an inferior person, to favor or bestow something to him and to be considerate often when it is not expected or deserved.

In addition, it came to pass the day after, that he went into a city called Nain; and many of his disciples went with him, and much people.

"Now when he came nigh to the gate of the city, behold, there was a dead man carried out, the only

son of his mother, and she was a widow: and much people of the city was with her. And when the Lord saw her, he had compassion on her, and said unto her, Weep not. And he came and touched the bier: and they that bare him stood still. And he said, Young man, I say unto thee, Arise. And he that was dead sat up, and began to speak. And he delivered him to his mother." Luke 7:12-15

When Jesus entered into the city of Nain, he met the youths near the gate of the city, going to bury a young boy, the only son of the mother. That not only, the woman had little or no opportunity to have another son as a widow, her son may have been killed in a wicked way. The power behind his death may have been human agents who wanted to keep this widow miserable all the days of her life. They must have planned how to deal with the widow. When Jesus saw how wickedly the devil and his agents had dealt with this woman, He had compassion on her.

Mercy, which is God's compassion, came not because the widow merited it. God's goodness upon the woman came by a deep tender feeling of compassion. The sight of wickedness and hopelessness that Jesus saw in the widow aroused it. When a suffering person presents himself to God and asks for His mercy, Jesus will be moved to have compassion. He will stoop kindness to release His mercy. The mercy of God is more powerful than death. It can stop the power of death at the gate, restore life to the weak, and deliver the weak from the powers that are stronger than he is.

The mercy of God can bring strength unto the weak, and raise the dead from death. It can restore your lost rights, benefits, and entitlements. It can cleanse your tears, comfort you, and quicken your mortal bodies. The mercy of God is forbearance towards someone in your power. It is getting involved in a matter beyond the rule or law to help the unworthy, helpless person.

"But my faithfulness and my mercy shall be with him: and in my name shall his horn be exalted. I will set his hand also in the sea, and his right hand in the rivers. He shall cry unto me, Thou art my father, my God, and the rock of my salvation. Also I will make him my firstborn, higher than the kings of the earth. My mercy will I keep for him for evermore, and my covenant shall stand fast with him. His seed also will I make to endure forever, and his throne as the days of heaven." Psalms 89:24-29.

God's mercy can lift up the down trodden, the rejected, and forsaken poor person. God's mercy can adopt the fatherless into God's family and make him God's firstborn, higher than earthly kings. When God's mercy is released unto someone, his level changes and he will live on earth as if he lives in heaven. When others are crying on earth for hardship, he will be rejoicing because his source is from heaven, not on earth. His Father is in heaven, not on earth. There is a measure of God's mercy you will receive that you will be on earth, but live as an ambassador on earth. The earth's problems and calamities will not touch you, because you are a stranger here.

When you obtain God's favor, you will not be afraid of problems, (even death), because your home is in heaven, your father is in heaven, your savior is in heaven, your name is in heaven. Your life, treasures, affections, heart, inheritance and citizenship is not on earth but in heaven.

God's mercy is God's specific, concrete acts of redemption in fulfilling of His promise. God's mercy is one of His most central characteristics offered to his people, who need redemption from sin, enemies and troubles. The grace of God can remove your guilt. With God's grace, you can endure misery, troubles, and problems. Nevertheless, if you receive God's mercy, your troubles, misery, problems are totally removed from you.

Chapter 2

WHO NEEDS GOD'S MERCY?

THE UNBELIEVERS, THE WEAK AND THE NEEDY

If you are weak spiritually or physically, you need to pray for God's mercy. If any area of your life is weak or under oppression, you should cry for God's mercy.

"Have mercy upon me, O LORD; for I am weak: O LORD, heal me; for my bones are vexed." Psalms 6:2

"Let us therefore come boldly unto the throne of grace that we may obtain mercy, and find grace to help in time of need." Hebrews 4:16

In times of need, you need to pray for God's mercy. A sinner - someone who is ignorant, an unbeliever - can obtain God's mercy to live right, and do God's work. If you want God's mercy to come upon a foolish person, disobedient person, deceived person, someone living in malice and envy, etc., God will answer. God's mercy when released, does not consider the magnitude of the victim's unrighteousness.

"For we ourselves also were sometimes foolish, disobedient, deceived, serving divers' lusts and pleasures, living in malice and envy, hateful, and hating one another. But after that the kindness and love of God our Savior toward man appeared, not by works of righteousness which we have done, but according to his mercy he saved us, by the washing of regeneration, and renewing of the Holy Ghost." Titus 3:3-5.

God's mercy can bring you out of any form of darkness, give you an office among His children, and make you a special person among others. When God separates you for His mercy, He will add you to his children to enjoy His divine, marvelous light.

"But ye are a chosen generation, a royal priesthood, an holy nation, a peculiar people; that ye should shew forth the praises of him who hath called you out of darkness into his marvelous light: Which in time past were not a people, but are now the people of God: which had not obtained mercy, but now have obtained mercy." 1Peter 2:9-10

God's mercy can remove you from among the defeated ones and place you among victorious people. It will come with a marvelous light that will expose all your darkness for destruction. In other words, if you are desolate, you need to pray for God's mercy. If you are under reproach, you need to pray for God's mercy. If you are under affliction, you need to pray for God's mercy. If you are a sinner, you need to pray for God's mercy. If you are sick, you need to pray for God's mercy.

The desolate can prayerfully ask God to turn to him with His mercy; the afflicted can also do the same. The troubled ones can also ask God for His divine mercy. There are many people who are in grief, powerless, and abandoned to suffer, yet they are not praying for God's mercy. If you need God's mercy, and you are praying for your enemies to die, you may never be delivered from your enemies. If you need God's mercy, and you are praying and fasting for prosperity, you may never prosper. If you need God's mercy and you are praying for marriage, you may never get married. When God's mercy comes, it comes with many good things.

There are many sinners, unbelievers, and wicked people, who are praying for their enemies to die, but they are wicked than their enemies. They fast for long, cry for provision, perfection, and breakthrough, but never get it. If they use the same strength to pray for God's mercy, they will be delivered. God's mercy covers many areas and makes our battle easy.

God's mercy can make God to be kind to you, shower His love on you, do you good, and have compassion on you. God may decide to leave your enemy alive, but give you more power than your enemy. He may not bring your enemy down, but can lift you higher than your enemy. He may not strike your enemy with stroke, but may empower your health wise, to be stronger than your enemy may. He may allow your enemy to be rich, but will make you richer than all your enemies put together. If God turns to you, and has mercy upon you, all your afflicters and enemies will bow. The mercy of God intimidates oppressors, troubles and troublers.

"Turn thee unto me, and have mercy upon me; for I am desolate and afflicted." Psalms 25:16.

"Have mercy upon me, O LORD, for I am in trouble: mine eye is consumed with grief, yea, my soul and my belly. For my life is spent with grief, and my years with sighing: my strength faileth because of mine iniquity, and my bones are consumed. I was a reproach among all mine enemies, but especially among my neighbors, and a fear to mine acquaintance: they that did see me without fled from me." Psalms 31:9-11

If you obtain God's mercy, your troubles will be terminated. If you obtain God's mercy, your grief will end. Nobody can be under God's mercy and the power behind his problem will stay for a moment, how much less the agent. The mercy of God comes with strength to destroy the power behind your problems, and reproach. Every other form of prayer may be acceptable, but prayer for mercy comes with God's presence without measure to deliver the oppressed.

"Sing, O heavens; and be joyful, O earth; and break forth into singing, O mountains: for the LORD hath comforted his people, and will have mercy upon his afflicted."　　Isaiah 49:13

"For the mountains shall depart, and the hills be removed; but my kindness shall not depart from thee, neither shall the covenant of my peace be removed, saith the LORD that hath mercy on thee. O thou afflicted, tossed with tempest, and not comforted, behold, I will lay thy stones with fair colors, and lay thy foundations with sapphires." Isaiah 54:10-11

"For we have not an high priest which cannot be touched with the feeling of our infirmities; but was in all points tempted like as we are, yet without sin. Let us therefore come boldly unto the throne of grace that we may obtain mercy, and find grace to help in time of need." Hebrews 4:15-16

The mercy of God brings songs in heaven, joy on earth, praises on mountains, and gives comfort to God's children. The reason why blessings come and go and deliverance comes and goes, is because many answers to some prayers do not have God's kindness. Kindness and mercy cannot be replaced no matter how powerful your enemies are. If you are under affliction, pray for God's mercy. If you are troubled, tossed up and down; pray for God's mercy. God's mercy can give you everlasting peace, long time praises and true freedom.

"And ye shall know the truth, and the truth shall make you free...If the Son therefore shall make you free, ye shall be free indeed." John 8:32, 36

Jesus is the physical mercy of God, sent by God to all humankind. He went about doing good, healing the sick, and delivering all that needed deliverance. If you are spiritually blind, and confused in life, pray for divine mercy. If you are physically blind, cry for divine mercy from the Master of mercy: God the Father, God the Son, and the Holy Ghost. Tell God to have mercy on you with all your heart and you will obtain mercy.

"And when Jesus departed thence, two blind men followed him, crying, and saying, Thou Son of David, have mercy on us. And when he was come into the house, the blind men came to him: and Jesus saith unto them,

believe ye that I am able to do this? They said unto him,
Yea, Lord. Then touched he their eyes, saying, according
to your faith be it unto you." Matthew. 9:27-29

If you want mercy from God, you must believe in
Jesus. You must have faith in Christ and His word.
When you believe in Christ and have faith in His
word, He will release His mercy unto you. Every
problem has a spirit behind it. At times, those
spirits may be a familiar spirit, invoked spirit, spirit
that comes through evil sacrifice, or evil groups that
people belonged to. The spirit may be ancestral,
residential, etc. However, no matter who is behind
your problem, if you pray for God's mercy in faith,
they must bow at the presence of God's mercy.

"Then Jesus went thence, and departed into the
coasts of Tyre and Sidon. And, behold, a woman

of Canaan came out of the same coasts, and cried unto him, saying, have mercy on me, O Lord, thou Son of David; my daughter is grievously vexed with a devil. But he answered her not a word. And his disciples came and besought him, saying, Send her away; for she crieth after us. But he answered and said, I am not sent but unto the lost sheep of the house of Israel. Then came she and worshipped him, saying, Lord, help me. But he answered and said, it is not meet to take the children's bread, and to cast it to dogs. And she said, Truth, Lord: yet the dogs eat of the crumbs which fall from their masters' table. Then Jesus answered and said unto her, O woman, great is thy faith: be it unto thee even as thou wilt. And her daughter was made whole from that very hour."

Matthew 15:21-28.

Occult people, family or territorial strongman, and household wickedness, are nothing at the manifestation of God's mercy. If you are seeking for God's mercy, you have to be consistent. You may even fast but you must also have faith in Christ and his words (Matthew. 17:18-20; 20:29-34; Mark 10:46-52; Luke 10:30-37). The land where you live and the land where you are born can receive divine mercy. If the land where you are born is under a curse, or where you live is under a curse, you can pray for God's mercy.

The land that needs God's mercy will affect its inhabitants. A land can attract God's wrath if the inhabitants go contrary to God's Word. In the days of Hosea, the inhabitant of the land polluted the land with lying, swearing, killing, stealing, committing adultery, etc. By so doing, they entered into controversy with God. Their land refused to yield increase and many kinds of evil spirits entered into the land, with all manner of problems. The land began to mourn, and all that lived in it started to languish, including the beast of the field, the fowls of heaven, and fishes of the sea. At that point, the land needed God's mercy.

> *"Hear the word of the LORD, ye children of Israel: for the LORD hath a controversy with the inhabitants of the land, because there is no truth, nor mercy, nor knowledge of God in the land. By swearing, and lying, and killing, and stealing, and committing adultery, they break out, and blood toucheth blood. Therefore, shall the land mourn, and every one that dwelleth therein shall languish, with the beasts of the field, and with the fowls of heaven; yea, the fishes of the sea also shall be taken away."* Hosea 4:1-3

The Lord can make a land to be empty and devoid of good things if the inhabitants pollute the place and refuse to repent. A land can be wasted, turned upside down, and the inhabitants scattered abroad, if the inhabitants pollute the place. Some countries may enter into war so that their land will drive them away if the inhabitant became abominable. When you see a country fighting, and rioting; and properties are being wasted, turned upside down, emptied of good things, utterly spoilt and faded away; it means the cup of their iniquity is full.

If a nation becomes haughty; filled with transgression, lawlessness, cheating and all manner of abomination; their land needs God's mercy. We need to pray for God's mercy in our land. Many nations are contending with factions, rebels, militants, and terrorists, because, the land needs mercy. If you do not pray for God's mercy in the land, there may be war, bloodshed, waste and all manner of confusion.

"Behold, the LORD maketh the earth empty, and maketh it waste, and turneth it upside down, and scattereth abroad the inhabitants thereof. And it shall be, as with the people, so with the priest; as with the servant, so with his master; as with the maid, so with her mistress; as with the buyer, so with the seller; as with the lender, so with the borrower; as with the taker of usury, so with the giver of usury to him. The land shall be utterly emptied, and utterly spoiled: for the LORD hath spoken this word. The earth mourneth and fadeth away, the world languisheth and fadeth away, the haughty people of the earth do languish. The earth also is defiled under the inhabitants thereof; because they have transgressed the laws, changed the ordinance, broken the everlasting covenant. Therefore, hath the curse devoured the earth, and they that dwell therein are desolate: therefore, the inhabitants of the earth are burned, and few men

left. The new wine mourneth, the vine languisheth, all the merry hearted do sigh. The mirth of tabretsceaseth, the noise of them that rejoice endeth, the joy of the harp ceaseth. They shall not drink wine with a song; strong drink shall be bitter to them that drink it. The city of confusion is broken down: every house is shut up, that no man may come in. There is a crying for wine in the streets; all joy is darkened, the mirth of the land is gone. In the city is left desolation, and the gate is smitten with destruction. When thus it shall be in the midst of the land among the people, there shall be as the shaking of an olive tree, and as the gleaning grapes when the vintage is done. They shall lift up their voice, they shall sing for the majesty of the LORD, they shall cry aloud from the sea. Wherefore glorify ye the LORD in the fires, even the name of the LORD God of Israel in the isles of the sea. From the uttermost part of the earth have we heard songs, even glory to the righteous. But I said, my leanness, my leanness, woe unto me! the treacherous dealers have dealt treacherously; yea, the treacherous dealers have dealt very treacherously. Fear, and the pit, and the snare, are upon thee, O inhabitant of the earth. And it shall come to pass, that he who fleeth from the noise of the fear shall fall into the pit; and he that cometh up out of the midst of the pit shall be taken in the snare: for the windows from on high are open, and the foundations of the earth do shake. The earth is utterly broken down, the earth is clean dissolved, the earth is moved exceedingly. The earth shall reel to and fro like a drunkard, and shall be removed like a cottage; and the transgression thereof shall be heavy upon it; and it shall fall, and not rise again. And it shall come to pass in that day, that the LORD shall punish the host of the high ones that are on high, and the kings of the earth upon the earth. And they shall be gathered together, as prisoners are gathered in the pit, and shall be shut up in the prison, and after many days shall they be visited. Then the moon shall be confounded, and the sun ashamed, when the LORD of hosts shall reign in mount Zion, and in Jerusalem, and before his ancients gloriously. "Isaiah 24:1-23

Many Lands if not prayed for, for God's mercy, will hear the noise of terror, fears, and shaking of their foundation. The land that is void of God's mercy shall be broken, cleaned, dissolved, and moved exceedingly. It shall reel to and fro like a drunkard, and be removed like a cottage. In the midst of these, their transgression will be heavy upon it and it shall fall and not rise.

You can see what is happening in the Middle East - the number of the refugees, deaths and destructions. Everyone is in trouble; the high up ones and the lowest are suffering. If we ignore to pray for God's mercy upon the land, peace will disappear and refuse to come back.

"Therefore seeing we have this ministry, as we have received mercy, we faint not; But have renounced the hidden things of dishonesty, not walking in craftiness, nor handling the word of God deceitfully; but by manifestation of the truth commending ourselves to every man's conscience in the sight of God." 2 Corinthians 4:1-2

"Now concerning virgins I have no commandment of the Lord: yet I give my judgment, as one that hath obtained mercy of the Lord to be faithful." 1 Corinthians 7:25

Even great ministers, who received their ministry from God, will not make it to the end if they do not pray for God's mercy. They will faint. Without God's mercy, many ministers will be dishonest, walk in craftiness, and handle God's work in deceit. They will not manifest in truth. Therefore, ministers of God need to pray for God's mercy. Those who love them should pray for God's mercy upon them, and not to gossip about them. If you obtain God's mercy, you can be faithful to work for God without fainting, being dishonest, walking in craftiness, or mishandling God's word. Ministers need God's mercy to keep the ministry they received from God. They need God's mercy to have clear conscience and to renounce the hidden things of dishonesty.

"Yet I supposed it necessary to send to you Epaphroditus, my brother, and companion in labor, and fellow soldier, but your messenger, and he that ministered to my wants. For he longed after you all, and was full of heaviness, because that ye had heard that he had been sick. For indeed he was sick nigh unto death: but God had mercy on him; and not on him only, but on me also, lest I should have sorrow upon sorrow. I sent him therefore the more carefully, that, when ye see him again, ye may rejoice, and that I may be the less sorrowful. Receive him therefore in the Lord with all gladness; and hold such in reputation: Because for the work of Christ he was nigh unto death, not regarding his life, to supply your lack of service toward me." Philippians 2:25-30

Some problems that come into ministers' lives are meant to destroy them if not for God's mercy. Lack of God's mercy has killed so many ministers of God. If the children of Israel had come together to pray for God's mercy on Moses, he may have been allowed by God to enter the Promised Land. When a minister loses God's mercy, his ministry may die. Some have backslidden, sought for help from lesser powers, and died in shame just because of the lack of God's mercy.

"And I thank Christ Jesus our Lord, who hath enabled me, for that he counted me faithful, putting me into the ministry." 1Timothy 1:12

"To Timothy, my dearly beloved son: Grace, mercy, and peace, from God the Father and Christ Jesus our Lord." 2Timothy 1:2

"To Titus, mine own son after the common faith: Grace, mercy, and peace, from God the Father and the Lord Jesus Christ our Savior." Titus 1:4

God's mercy is a very vital. Though most Christians neglect or are not aware of its importance, so they do not pray for it. The unbelievers, the weak, the needy, the desolate, reproachful sinners, and the inhabitants of the land, have lost many blessings for not praying for God's mercy. Many ministers called by God have lived and died without achieving much, because they did not pray for God's mercy. Many of our loved ones, and even leaders, have died unfulfilled, because nobody saw the need to pray for God's mercy on their behalf.

Paul the apostle knew that his son in the Lord, Timothy, needed God's mercy to fulfil his ministry, and he prayed for him. There will be a great change when we begin to pray for God's mercy on earth. Mercy of God brings peace from God, the Father of our Lord, Jesus Christ. All the people who worked with and were prayed for by Paul received God's mercy to fulfil their calling except a few.

"And as many as walk according to this rule, peace be on them, and mercy, and upon the Israel of God." Galatians 6:16.

"But ye, beloved, building up yourselves on your most holy faith, praying in the Holy Ghost, keep yourselves in the love of God, looking for the mercy of our Lord Jesus Christ unto eternal life." Jude 20-21.

Even the children of God who walked according to the law of God, need God's mercy. God's children who are holy, faithful, and spirit-filled, need God's mercy until they reach their Promised Land. Therefore, no matter your position on earth, and who you are, you need God's mercy. Your position determines the kind of mercy you need. Unbelievers, the weak, the needy, the desolate, reproachful, afflicted, sinners, the sick, the land, the ministers, and even God's children, all need God's mercy in different ways. The area you need mercy is different from the area another person needs mercy. Some mercies that come from God may take you away from the dominating powers of Goliath, destroy your weakness, provide your needs; take you away from isolation, shame, disgrace, sickness, curse, ministerial failure and any problem of life. If you pray for mercy you will receive God's love, goodness, kindness, pity, and compassion; and you will be removed or delivered from misery.

Chapter 3

THE POWER OF GOD'S MERCY

The mercy of God comes from heaven with enough power to displace any power in place. Because it comes from above, it is above every satanic activity on earth; with everything you need to succeed in life. The habitation of God's mercy is holiness and divine glory. When God releases His mercy on earth, it comes with zeal to perform God's command. The sounding of God's mercy comes with an overwhelming strength and cannot be stopped or restrained from performing God's command.

"Look down from heaven, and behold from the habitation of thy holiness and of thy glory: where is thy zeal and thy strength, the sounding of thy bowels and of thy mercies toward me? Are they restrained?" Isaiah 63:15.

"Thou in thy mercy hast led forth the people which thou hast redeemed: thou hast guided them in thy strength unto thy holy habitation." Exodus 15:13.

"The LORD is longsuffering, and of great mercy, forgiving iniquity and transgression, and by no means clearing the guilty, visiting the iniquity of

the fathers upon the children unto the third and fourth generation. Pardon, I beseech thee, the iniquity of this people according unto the greatness of thy mercy, and as thou hast forgiven this people, from Egypt even until now." Numbers 14:18-19.

With all the powers of Egypt in the time of Pharaoh, he could not stop the children of Israel from moving out of bondage. God's mercy is accompanied with every power needed to set the captives free. The determination of an enemy may last when God's mercy is not available. No matter your situations, if you plead for God's mercy, the powers behind your problems must surrender. In times of God's mercy, redemption is made easy. In the presence of God's mercy, there is no lack of power to achieve greatness.

God's mercy when released, guides the victims in the midst of their problems, oppressors and destructive enemies, unto a safe place at their habitation. If God's mercy defiled the power of all the Egyptian gods and their magicians, the same power can take you away from your problems. All believers deserve God's mercy and are qualified to plead for it. In addition, no matter how wicked you are, if you repent and turn to God, His mercy will locate you. The reason why many wicked people are alive is that God wants to extend His mercy unto them. That is what we call the longsuffering of God.

The scriptures call God's mercy great, because through His mercy, sinners, no matter how sinful and wicked, can be forgiven at God's mercy. When God's mercy is released unto a sinner, iniquity and transgression flee away in a moment of time. Every satanic work is so afraid when they feel the presence of God's mercy. At God's mercy, guilt can be cleared, respecting God's mercy to do its work. Sin, iniquity and transgression in the absence of God's mercy can present someone's iniquity; that of his ancestors; to destroy even to the third and fourth generation.

A wise person, family, community, or nation, repents and pleads for God's mercy. If you ask for God's pardon as a sinner, repent and forsake your sins, the great mercy of God will appear in the battlefield for your sake. Your sin can be many; your ancestral abomination may mount to Heaven. However, they cannot work against you at God's great mercy. The powers of the devil, forces of darkness, and multitudes of problems are helpless at the manifestation of God's mercy. Most people think they need money, wealth, and pleasure. Nevertheless, what they really need is God's mercy. God's mercy when released carries every human need and brings solutions.

"And he said, LORD God of Israel, there is no God like thee, in heaven above, or on earth beneath, who keepest covenant and mercy with thy servants that walk before thee with all their heart: Who hast kept with thy servant David my father that thou promises him: thou spakest also with thy mouth, and hast fulfilled it with thine hand, as it is this day." 1 Kings 8:23-24.

"Thou which hast kept with thy servant David my father that which thou hast promised him; and spakest with thy mouth, and hast fulfilled it with thine hand, as it is this day." 2 Chronicles 6:15

"And when he had consulted with the people, he appointed singers unto the LORD, and that

should praise the beauty of holiness, as they went out before the army, and to say, Praise the LORD; for his mercy endureth forever. And when they began to sing and to praise, the LORD set ambushments against the children of Ammon, Moab, and mount Seir, which were come against Judah; and they were smitten." 2 Chronicles 20:21-22.

God's mercy distinguishes God from gods, and belittles every evil force, including the devil. Satan can show his power where there is no divine mercy. The scarcity of divine mercy on earth is the reason for all the sufferings and misery we see everywhere. If you want God's mercy, repent, keep His covenants, and walk before Him with all your heart. When there is no mercy of God in a person's life, place or thing, the promise of God will not manifest, no matter how much you pray.

Many deliverance candidates do not know that what they need is God's mercy to receive their deliverance. Good things come and go (even deliverance) in the absent of God's mercy. God's mercy guides jealously what God provides for His people, and scares problems away. Every word that comes out of God's mouth brings the result when God's mercy manifests. God's promises can only manifest when his mercy is recognized and asked for. Songs of praise and prayers can attract God's presence; but what causes God to manifest his power is his mercy. God's mercy can endure; stay, and work, until the host of enemies flee. That was what king David enjoyed when he testifies that God's mercy endures forever. Prayers and praises can attract God's presence, if you add prayers to your work and praise Him from your inner heart. These can extend God's mercy to you and people around you. It can strengthen you and cause His hand to remain upon you. His mercy can link you up everywhere you go in life with people that matter in the society to serve you.

"But I will sing of thy power; yea, I will sing aloud of thy mercy in the morning: for thou hast been my defence and refuge in the day of my trouble. Unto thee, O my strength, will I sing: for God is my defence, and the God of my mercy." Psalms 59:16-17.

"O turn unto me, and have mercy upon me; give thy strength unto thy servant, and save the son of thine handmaid." Psalms 86:16.

When you receive God's mercy, no matter how sorrowful you were before, you will be forced to sing aloud in the presence of your enemies. The remembrance of deliverance from the hands of your oppressors will compel you to wake up with songs of praise. God's mercy does not only destroy your misery, sorrows and problems; it brings defence to the defenseless, and refuge in the day of trouble. One who receives God's mercy can be comfortable anywhere on earth. When God's mercy appears in your battlefield to deliver you, it comes along with His glory and enough power. Your prayers can cause God to visit your battlefield, and turn towards you. However, without God's mercy, you will not have power over your enemies. The enemy may run away at God's presence but may return latter to resume His work. God's mercy delivers you, keeps you out of trouble, and brings you to your place of abode.

"I have found David my servant; with my holy oil have I anointed him: With whom my hand shall

be established: mine arm also shall strengthen him. The enemy shall not exact upon him; nor the son of wickedness afflict him. And I will beat down his foes before his face, and plague them that hate him. But my faithfulness and my mercy shall be with him: and in my name shall his horn be exalted. I will set his hand also in the sea, and his right hand in the rivers. He shall cry unto me, Thou art my father, my God, and the rock of my salvation. Also I will make him my firstborn, higher than the kings of the earth. My mercy will I keep for him for evermore, and my covenant shall stand fast with him. His seed also will I make to endure forever, and his throne as the days of heaven." Psalms 89:20-29.

When the mercy of God located David, everything about him changed. He was anointed with God's oil from heaven. The mercy of God helped him to be established, and he was strengthened above all his enemies. God's mercy will not allow its candidate to be exacted by his enemies, nor will it allow the son of wickedness afflict him. God's mercy brings every enemy down, and plagues all that hate you. Once you pray down God's mercy, God will appear and be with you. If you receive healing, blessings, and deliverance without God's mercy, they may not stay long. Nevertheless, God's mercy faithfully gives you deliverance, and gives it to the end.

God's mercy brings promotion, expands your coast, and causes you to be favored everywhere. God's mercy can present you before people and introduce you as God's own person. When God's mercy manifests on your behalf, you will be promoted above your masters. That was what David enjoyed all his life and he never lost any battle. If you pray and secure God's mercy, your children will never be put to shame or suffer lack of divine help. God's mercy is filled with life that cannot fade away or be expired.

"To him who alone doeth great wonders: for his mercy endureth forever. To him that by wisdom made the heavens: for his mercy endureth forever. To him that stretched out the earth above the waters: for his mercy endureth forever. To him that made great lights: for his mercy endureth for ever: The sun to rule by day: for his mercy endureth for ever: The moon and stars to rule by night: for his mercy endureth forever. To him that smote Egypt in their firstborn: for his mercy endureth for ever: And brought out Israel from among them: for his mercy endureth for ever: With a strong hand, and with a stretched out arm: for his mercy endureth forever. To him which divided the Red sea into parts: for his mercy endureth for ever: And made Israel to pass

through the midst of it: for his mercy endureth for ever: But overthrew Pharaoh and his host in the Red sea: for his mercy endureth forever. To him which led his people through the wilderness: for his mercy endureth forever. To him which smote great kings: for his mercy endureth for ever: And slew famous kings: for his mercy endureth for ever: Sihon king of the Amorites: for his mercy endureth for ever: And Og the king of Bashan: for his mercy endureth for ever:" Psalms 136:4-20.

God's mercy brings wonders, wisdom, expansion, blessings; it sheds great light, wastes enemies, breaks captivities, and makes a way where there is no way. God's mercy promotes people to the next level, overthrows their enemies, removes confusion, disgraces evil geniuses, brings evil famous men down, and settles God's children down in safety without troubles.

"And I will strengthen the house of Judah, and I will save the house of Joseph, and I will bring them again to place them; for I have mercy upon them: and they shall be as though I had not cast them off: for I am the LORD their God, and will hear them. And they of Ephraim shall be like a mighty man, and their heart shall rejoice as through wine: yea, their children shall see it, and be glad; their heart shall rejoice in the LORD." Zechariah. 10:6-7.

The mercy of God can supply every need, feed the hungry, enrich the poor, and blesses him to forget all his past sufferings. No matter how weak you are, if you receive God's mercy, your might will increase until you become a mighty person. God's mercy brings joy right inside the heart, and all the people around will see it and rejoice with you. The mercy of God turns the captivity captives and draws sinners close to God. It makes people to testify of God's goodness, and decamp from evil camps. You need God's mercy urgently; that is the need of our generation. Ask God for his mercy that endures forever and He will give it to you. Unless you repent and forsake your sins, the mercy of God will not clear your guilt nor be blind to your sins.

"And the LORD passed by before him, and proclaimed, The LORD, The LORD God, merciful and gracious, longsuffering, and abundant in goodness and truth, Keeping mercy for thousands, forgiving iniquity and transgression and sin, and that will by no means clear the guilty; visiting the iniquity of the fathers upon the children, and upon the children's

children, unto the third and to the fourth generation." Exodus 34:6-7.

"The LORD is longsuffering, and of great mercy, forgiving iniquity and transgression, and by no means clearing the guilty, visiting the iniquity of the fathers upon the children unto the third and fourth generation...How long shall I bear with this evil congregation, which murmur against me? I have heard the murmurings of the children of Israel, which they murmur against me." Numbers. 14:18,27.

Even if you receive God's mercy, compassion and goodness, and you do not repent and forsake your sins, He will not clear you from guilt. Because of God's kindness, love, deep tender feelings and compassion, He may be aroused by the sight of your weakness, and suffering; stooping to consider you for mercy. But He will not clear your iniquity or guilt if you do not truly repent.

You may enjoy God's mercy for long; your generation may receive God's mercy for thousands of years. However, if they do not repent and turn away from their sins, their iniquity must be visited and their guilt not cleared, no matter how long it takes. The only condition to receive God's mercy and enjoy it is to repent thoroughly and truly. If you repent, God will forgive you of all your iniquities and transgressions, and clear your guilt.

"Know therefore that the LORD thy God, he is God, the faithful God, which keepeth covenant and mercy with them that love him and keep his commandments to a thousand generations; And repayment them that hate him to their face, to

destroy them: he will not be slack to him that hadeeth him, he will repay him to his face."
Deuteronomy. 7:9-10

"And when thy days be fulfilled, and thou shalt sleep with thy fathers, I will set up thy seed after thee, which shall proceed out of thy bowels, and I will establish his kingdom. He shall build an house for my name, and I will stablish the throne of his kingdom forever. I will be his father, and he shall be my son. If he commit iniquity, I will chasten him with the rod of men, and with the stripes of the children of men: But my mercy shall not depart away from him, as I took it from Saul, whom I put away before thee. And thine house and thy kingdom shall be established for ever before thee: thy throne shall be established forever." 2 Samuel 7:12-16.

God's mercy works by keeping His covenant. You are qualified for God's mercy. Qualification to God's mercy does not automatically release it; you may need to provoke it. Show God that you need it, and pray for it. If someone that hates God attacks you (a covenant breaker), God will repay him if he does not repent. The God you serve is not afraid of any power and their problems. If you obtain God's mercy, it will outlive you and be extended to your children. The greatest investment and help you will give your children, or leave behind for them is not money, property, or material things. It is keeping God's commandment and obtaining His mercy. If you obtain God's mercy, you will fulfil your destiny on earth and your days will be blessed. The greatest achievement on earth is to repent, confess your sins, forsake them, and obtain God's mercy. Whatever it will take you, it is worth it.

"For David, after he had served his own generation by the will of God, fell on sleep, and was laid unto his fathers, and saw corruption:"
Acts 13:36

David faced many battles to please God and obtain His mercy. After his life on earth, his children enjoyed God's mercy. They were established in their father's given kingdom. They lived and did what their father could not do. All through King Solomon's reign, God was with him not because of his righteousness, but because his father obtained God's mercy. Though Solomon was not above God's chastisement each time he committed iniquity, but God's mercy never departed from him unto death. This was because of his father's foundation of divine mercy.

At times, God deals with us according to our foundation. Nevertheless, if you are serious, you can move out from any bad foundation and start a new one with God today. It is possible through true repentance. The worst thing that can happen to anyone is for God to take away his mercy from you. If Satan does a thing, it will not last. However, when it is God, you need to seek for his assistance for restoration. Sin can cause God's mercy to be present without action, but may never remove you permanently. That is why you can stand upon the precious shed blood of Jesus and provoke God's mercy now and it will manifest.

"My mercy will I keep for him for evermore, and my covenant shall stand fast with him. His seed also will I make to endure forever, and his throne as the days of heaven. If his children forsake my law, and walk not in my judgments; If they break

*my statutes, and keep not my commandments;
Then will I visit their transgression with the rod,
and their iniquity with stripes. Nevertheless, my
loving kindness will I not utterly take from him,
nor suffer my faithfulness to fail."* Psalms 89:28-
33

God keeps His mercy in a life, place, or thing
forever, and no power can tamper with it. If you are
not experiencing God's mercy, you can quicken or
provoke it by keeping God's covenant. The death
and resurrection of Jesus on the cross of Calvary has
brought everyone, who repents under God's mercy.
But it can be provoked by the way you live your
life, work for God, pray to God and praise Him. As
a believer, breaking God's law can expose you to
satanic attacks and silence God's mercy.
Nevertheless, you can provoke it by repentance,

forsaking your sins and keeping God's covenant again.

No one on earth who believes in Christ and loves God can ever be denied access to God's mercy. You can receive God's mercy, if you give your life to Christ today. You can receive God's mercy if you return to God and keep His covenants.

"The word of the LORD that came unto Hosea, the son of Beeri, in the days of Uzziah, Jotham, Ahaz, and Hezekiah, kings of Judah, and in the days of Jeroboam the son of Joash, king of Israel...And the LORD said unto him, call his name Jezreel; for yet a little while, and I will avenge the blood of Jezreel upon the house of Jehu, and will cause to cease the kingdom of the house of Israel. And it shall come to pass at that day, that I

will break the bow of Israel in the valley of Jezreel." Hosea 1:1; 4-5.

If you love someone and want him to obtain God's mercy and enjoy the good things of life from God, plead with Him to repent and keep God's covenant. No matter how determined you are to help a person, if he is not born again, your help is just temporary.

Chapter 4

THE POSITION OF GOD'S MERCY

In the kingdom rankings, mercy has a position apportioned to it by the scriptures. When you search the scriptures, you will discover that God's mercy is higher than purpose in the kingdom rankings.

"And, behold, a woman of Canaan came out of the same coasts, and cried unto him, saying, have mercy on me, O Lord, thou Son of David; my daughter is grievously vexed with a devil. However, he answered her not a word. And his disciples came and besought him, saying, Send her away; for she crieth after us. But he answered and said, I am not sent but unto the lost sheep of the house of Israel. Then came she and worshipped him, saying, Lord, help me. But he answered and said, it is not meet to take the children's bread, and to cast it to dogs. And she said, Truth, Lord: yet the dogs eat of the crumbs which fall from their masters' table. Then Jesus answered and said unto her, O woman, great is thy faith: be it unto thee even as thou wilt. And her daughter was made whole from that very hour." Matthew. 15:22-28.

When Jesus entered into one of the coasts of Tyre and Sidon, He met a woman who demanded for mercy on behalf of her daughter. His main purpose was to minister to the lost sheep of the house of Israel. But when this woman by faith confronted Him, demanding for mercy first, Jesus postponed his original purpose.

"For he saith to Moses, I will have mercy on whom I will have mercy, and I will have compassion on whom I will have compassion. So then it is not of him that willeth, nor of him that runneth, but of God that sheweth mercy. For the scripture saith unto Pharaoh, even for this same purpose have I raised thee up, that I might shew my power in thee, and that my name might be declared throughout all the earth. Therefore, hath he mercy on whom he will have mercy, and whom he will he hardeneth. Thou wilt say then unto me,

why doth he yet finds fault? For who hath resisted his will? Nay but, O man, who art thou that repliest against God? Shall the thing formed say to him that formed it, why hast thou made me thus? Hath not the potter power over the clay, of the same lump to make one vessel unto honor, and another unto dishonor? What if God, willing to shew his wrath, and to make his power known, endured with much longsuffering the vessels of wrath fitted to destruction: And that he might make known the riches of his glory on the vessels of mercy, which he had afore prepared unto glory"
Romans. 9:15-23.

The mercy of God, which is God's kindness, pity and compassion, rules over God's purpose if you demand it consistently by faith. Jesus can abandon your shortcomings and release his mercies upon you if in praise and faith you provoke Him to do so.

When God is contacted by faith through prayer, He can be aroused by the sight of your weakness, suffering, and pains; abandoning everything to stoop in kindness to have mercy on you. When an enemy is raised to torment you, it is for a purpose. But if in your pains, suffering and weakness, you cry to God for his mercy, He can ignore His purpose and have mercy upon you. Your problems may defy every other power, but at the release of divine mercy, no power; not even the purpose for which you are suffering can stand.

Even in this situation of suffering that you may be experiencing, God wants to show you mercy, and demonstrate His power over your problems and the power behind it. God can ignore His own purpose to which He allowed your enemies over your life and release His mercy above His original purpose. Pharaoh with all his occult witchcraft powers, even with God's support, could not stand God's mercy for the children of Israel. Therefore, no matter the purpose to which you are suffering, God can ignore it and have mercy upon you if you pray in faith. God's mercy does not come alone; it comes with every power to overthrow every power backing your problems. You may be faulty, guilty, or sinful. Nevertheless, God's mercy overrules all these if you pray with readiness to forsake your sin and start living right. God has all manner of vessels, which He has prepared to pour His mercy upon you if you make a demand.

"And I thank Christ Jesus our Lord, who hath enabled me, for that he counted me faithful, putting me into the ministry; Who was before a blasphemer, and a persecutor, and injurious: but I obtained mercy, because I did it ignorantly in unbelief. And the grace of our Lord was exceeding abundant with faith and love which is in Christ Jesus. This is a faithful saying, and worthy of all

acceptation, that Christ Jesus came into the world to save sinners; of whom I am chief. Howbeit for this cause I obtained mercy, that in me first Jesus Christ might shew forth all longsuffering, for a pattern to them which should hereafter believe on him to life everlasting." 1Timothy 1:12-16

"But ye are a chosen generation, a royal priesthood, an holy nation, a peculiar people; that ye should shew forth the praises of him who hath called you out of darkness into his marvelous light: Which in time past were not a people, but are now the people of God: which had not obtained mercy, but now have obtained mercy." 1Peter 2:9-10

You may be the worst sinner - an armed robber, the worst of all the worse on earth. But if you obtain

God's mercy, you will escape from every bondage. God's mercy can destroy every evil purpose and enable you to fulfil the purpose for which you were created. When you obtain God's mercy, you will be counted worthy, and faithful to handle God's programs. No matter how your life injured people of God before, God's mercy can remove all those things against you and declare you worthy to be accepted before God as if you never committed sin, if you truly repent and forsake your sins to God. You may be in darkness; under the control of the devil. But when God's mercy appears for your sake, you will receive God's marvelous light to see and escape every bondage. God's favor can adopt you, remove you from every problem and make you an acceptable child of God.

"Thou therefore, O LORD God of hosts, the God of Israel, awake to visit all the heathen: be not

merciful to any wicked transgressors. Selah. They return at evening: they make a noise like a dog, and go round about the city. Behold, they belch out with their mouth: swords are in their lips: for who, say they, doth hear? But thou, O LORD, shalt laugh at them; thou shalt have all the heathen in derision. Because of his strength will I wait upon thee: for God is my defence. The God of my mercy shall prevent me: God shall let me see my desire upon mine enemies. Slay them not, lest my people forget: scatter them by thy power; and bring them down, O Lord our shield. For the sin of their mouth and the words of their lips let them even be taken in their pride: and for cursing and lying which they speak. Consume them in wrath, consume them, that they may not be: and let them know that God ruleth in Jacob unto the ends of the earth. Selah." Psalms 59:5-13.

There are things that can naturally take place if you receive divine mercy. At the presence of divine mercy, God will awake, arise, and visit all the enemies against you. When God visits your enemy, the wicked; He offers them two things: one, salvation. Two; reward for their evil against you, if they reject salvation. So even if you pray for the death of your enemies or not, when God in His mercy arises for your sake, every purpose against you will submit and bow. All evil noise, sword of the wicked, and their laughter over you will cease. You will see your desires over your enemy's manifest. God's mercies can scatter your enemies, overthrow them, bring them down, consume them in wrath, and bring their works and purpose over you to an end.

"And when they had gone through the isle unto Paphos, they found a certain sorcerer, a false

prophet, a Jew, whose name was Bar Jesus: Which was with the deputy of the country, Sergius Paulus, a prudent man; who called for Barnabas and Saul, and desired to hear the word of God. But Elymas the sorcerer (for so is his name by interpretation) withstood them, seeking to turn away the deputy from the faith. Then Saul, (who also is called Paul,) filled with the Holy Ghost, set his eyes on him, and said, O full of all subtlety and all mischief, thou child of the devil, thou enemy of all righteousness, wilt thou not cease to pervert the right ways of the Lord? And now, behold, the hand of the Lord is upon thee, and thou shalt be blind, not seeing the sun for a season. And immediately there fell on him a mist and a darkness; and he went about seeking some to lead him by the hand. Then the deputy, when he saw what was done, believed, being astonished at the doctrine of the Lord." Acts 13:6-12.

At God's mercy, the purpose of every sorcerer, false prophets, and wicked people will be put to naught. No occult person can successfully withstand a favored person, no matter their purpose. If God can ignore His own purpose to give you mercy, no evil purpose will stand when God's mercy appears for your sake. The purpose of Elymas the sorcerer over Sergius Paulus was defeated at God's mercy. Though the sorcerer was full of evil powers, subtlety, and mischief, all those bowed at God's mercy. He was the child of the devil; an enemy of righteousness, who for so long a time, refused to cease from perverting the right ways of God. Because of this, at the appearance of God's mercy, he suddenly became blind because a mist and darkness fell on him. You may not need to waste time praying for the death of your enemies or against their evil purpose. You need to cry to God for his mercy. This is because at God's mercy, the un-repented, wicked ones will be judged. The righteous is vindicated, delivered, and promoted above their enemies. So, pray for God's mercy. Provoke God's mercy, and remain faithful to His word, no matter your situation. God's mercy is higher than purpose.

Again, God's mercy is higher in rank than faith. Faith is a great instrument to receive answers to prayers. It is very powerful because without it no one can please God. But in position, God's mercy is higher in ranking.

"For as ye in times past have not believed God, yet have now obtained mercy through their unbelief: Even so have these also now not believed, that through your mercy they also may obtain mercy. For God hath concluded them all in unbelief, that he might have mercy upon all." Romans. 11:30-32.

There are things you may never get if you do not have faith. There are levels you may never reach if you do not believe in God. If you pray to God and obtain mercy, all things may be possible. You can obtain mercy even in your unbelief as God moves by His compassion and loving kindness.

Unbelievers, sinners or saints can obtain God's mercy in the midst a great multitude if they can cry for it. Your prayer for mercy can attract Jesus to show mercy on you, no matter how sinful or wicked you are.

"And as they departed from Jericho, a great multitude followed him. And, behold, two blind men sitting by the way side, when they heard that Jesus passed by, cried out, saying, Have mercy on us, O Lord, thou Son of David. And the multitude rebuked them, because they should hold their

peace: but they cried the more, saying, Have mercy on us, O Lord, thou Son of David. And Jesus stood still, and called them, and said, what will ye that I shall do unto you? They say unto him, Lord, that our eyes may be opened. So Jesus had compassion on them, and touched their eyes: and immediately their eyes received sight, and they followed him."
Matthew. 20:29-34.

There are many believers who are following Christ; working for Him and with Him, but they suffer in silence. Some cry and pray, but they are not serious or determined to receive change. When Jesus was leaving Jericho His purpose was different. You can follow Christ for life, have faith in Him but not obtain mercy. Jesus ignored a great multitude that had faith in Him and followed Him from Jericho to extend His mercy unto the two blind men sitting by the wayside. When these two blind men specifically cried out to Jesus for mercy, He was touched with pity and compassion; and the sight of their suffering aroused him. He stoops down in kindness and releases mercy on them. Many people have faith in Christ but never cried out enough, they lived without obtaining mercy. Even if you have faith in Christ, without crying and praying for divine mercy to attract Christ, you may never enjoy God's mercy. If you hold your peace, enduring your reproach, shame and disgrace, without being seriously determined to obtain mercy, you may lack God's loving kindness, goodness and compassion to an extent. Therefore, knowing Christ, having faith in Him, and following Him from Jericho (place to place) may not secure God's mercy if you do not provoke it. The two blind men cried out for mercy and Jesus considered them, though they were inferior to those who followed Him from Jericho. Mercy is higher than faith because it can cause Jesus to have deep and tender feeling toward an inferior person. Mercy moved Him to help the undeserving, and with pity also.

A sinner who knows how to cry for mercy can attract divine attention. God's mercy can attract divine attention. At God's kindness, the faithless, and the sinful can change his mind and follow Christ today. If you have followed Christ from Jericho (place to place), you have the right to set time aside, sit down, and start crying for divine mercy. It is very bad to follow Christ, work for Him and with Him, yet you lack divine mercy, while strangers around you provoke God's mercy all the time. As a believer, you need God's kindness, favor, and mercy; and He is willing and happy to release it if you pray.

"But go ye and learn what that meaneth, I will have mercy, and not sacrifice: for I am not come to

call the righteous, but sinners to repentance."
Matthew. 9:13

"But if ye had known what *this* meaneth, I
will have mercy, and not sacrifice, ye would
not have condemned the guiltless." Matthew.
12:7.

God's mercy cannot be obtained by sacrifice. His
mercy is higher than sacrifice. There are good things
you may never enjoy by sacrifice, working for God,
or doing good. Until you move God through direct
prayers for mercy, you may never enjoy all that He
has for you. This is why you can put much sacrifice
to serve God, but an unbeliever may move God by
his cry to feel for him and release His mercy. Being
righteous or doing exploits for God without directly
seeking for his mercy may deny you many of God's

blessings. You must show God that you have the need of mercy in addition to your sacrifices in His kingdom. Believers have more right and are fit for God's mercy than others but they have to provoke it. Cry for it and God will be moved to release it.

"And he marvelled because of their unbelief. And he went round about the villages, teaching. And he called unto him the twelve, and began to send them forth by two and two; and gave them power over unclean spirits; And commanded them that they should take nothing for their journey, save a staff only; no scrip, no bread, no money in their purse:" Mark 6:6-8.

The problem is that many believers are more familiar with God. That is the reason why many are not enjoying his mercy. Jesus could not release His mercy more among his own kin and his own house because they were so familiar with Him. You may keep God's law and return your tithes; but if you don't show Christ your need for His mercy, you may die without mercy.

"Woe unto you, scribes and Pharisees, hypocrites! for ye pay tithe of mint and anise and cummin, and have omitted the weightier matters of the law, judgment, mercy, and faith: these ought ye to have done, and not to leave the other undone." Matthew. 23:23.

"Thy mercy, O LORD, is in the heavens; and thy faithfulness reacheth unto the clouds." Psalms 36:5.

The Pharisees and scribes were destined to obtain mercy from God and distribute it to others; but they failed! Though they paid tithes of mint and anise and cumin, they omitted the weightier matters of the law, which is mercy. The mercy of God is higher than tithes, heavens, and height of heavens. God's mercy comes directly from heaven and does not submit to lower powers. His mercy is so great and higher than the heights of heavens. Every problem, earthly powers, and the elemental forces bow at the presence of God's mercy.

"For as the heaven is high above the earth, so great is his mercy toward them that fear him." Psalms 103: 11

"For thy mercy is great above the heavens: and thy truth reacheth unto the clouds." Psalms 108:4.

As the heaven is higher above the earth, so is God's mercy higher than any power on earth. The mercy of God can make its benefactor great upon the earth. If you want to live above every power of darkness and its problems on earth, seek for God's mercy. Do you know that at the appearance of God's mercy, He can go change His word?

"And thou shalt put the mercy seat above upon the ark; and in the ark thou shalt put the testimony that I shall give thee. And there I will meet with thee, and I will commune with thee from above the mercy seat, from between the two cherubims which are upon the ark of the testimony, of all things which I will give thee in commandment unto the children of Israel. "Exodus 25:21-22

"And thou shalt put the mercy seat upon the ark of the testimony in the most holy place." Exodus 26:34

The ark of God contains God's word, but God mandated Mosses to put his mercy seat above the ark. If you obtain God's mercy, you have secured God's full presence; and at that point, anything can happen to your favor. If a sinner can insist and get God's mercy even when God's word oppose it, then a believer, a true child of God can get much more. Jesus went ahead contrary to the custom and had mercy upon a woman of Canaan.

"Then was brought unto him one possessed with a devil, blind, and dumb: and he healed him, insomuch that the blind and dumb both spake and saw. And all the people were amazed, and said, Is

not this the son of David? But when the Pharisees heard it, they said, this fellow doth not cast out devils, but by Beelzebub the prince of the devils. And Jesus knew their thoughts, and said unto them, every kingdom divided against itself is brought to desolation; and every city or house divided against itself shall not stand: And if Satan cast out Satan, he is divided against himself; how shall then his kingdom stand? And if I by Beelzebub cast out devils, by whom do your children cast them out? therefore they shall be your judges. But if I cast out devils by the Spirit of God, then the kingdom of God is come unto you." Matthew.12:22-28.

Whenever there is need for mercy, Jesus can go contrary to his word to release it, even on Sabbath days (Matthew 12:1-8 9:10-13 Mark 1:40-45. Hebrews 44:16). Lepers forbidden and isolated by

God's word received God's mercy. If you are born again, you have more rights than sinners. The woman of Canaan obtained God's mercy. You are therefore, invited to come boldly in prayer unto the throne of grace to obtain mercy and grace to be helped in times of need.

Chapter 5

PURPOSE OF GOD'S MERCY

God has a purpose in everything in life, and one of his major purpose of mercy is to save His name and protect His integrity.

"But do thou for me, O GOD the Lord, for thy name's sake: because thy mercy is good, deliver thou me." Psalms 109:21

"Not unto us, O LORD, not unto us, but unto thy name give glory, for thy mercy, and for thy truth's sake." Psalms 115:1.

"Therefore thus saith the Lord GOD; Now will I bring again the captivity of Jacob, and have mercy upon the whole house of Israel, and will be jealous for my holy name;" Ezekiel 39:25.

God may not want to do something but if His name is at stake, He may decide to render His mercy to save His name. Most deliverance that people receive from God, especially those who have relationship with Him is to save His name and protect His integrity. So you can plead for God's mercy not because you are qualified or merit it but because of His name. If God is sure that His glory will be returned to Him, He may decide to release

His mercy. If you convince God that you will not take His glory or give it to another, He will have mercy on you and deliver you from whatever trouble or problem you find yourself. You should not base your prayers of your deliverance on your righteousness, service, or ability to pray and fast. That is why many people pray so long, fast, sow seeds, but they are not delivered.

I have often heard people complain that they have prayed all manner of prayers; fasted so much, and done all kinds of things but they were not delivered. God is so jealous that he cannot share His glory with anyone. Most deliverance ministers, prayer contractors, and godfathers have diverted God's glory. That is why many prayers are no longer being answered. Every glory for whatever thing we do must go to God and not to man or idol. If you want God's mercy for true deliverance, give all glory to God. If you give God all the glory from your heart, He will show you mercy.

"O Lord, hear; O Lord, forgive; O Lord, hearken and do; defer not, for thine own sake, O my God: for thy city and thy people are called by thy name." Daniel 9:19.

"Return, O LORD, deliver my soul: oh save me for thy mercies' sake." Psalms 6:4.

If you are captured, oppressed, or see yourself in any kind of problem, God expects you to run to Him. If you sincerely repent from your heart, God's name will be at stake, and He will surely deliver you to save His name. Many people's repentance is not genuine from their hearts. They are not fully with God; yet they pray, fast, and try to force God to answer their prayers and deliver them.

"And the statutes, and the ordinances, and the law, and the commandment, which he wrote for you, ye shall observe to do for evermore; and ye shall not fear other gods. And the covenant that I have made with you ye shall not forget; neither shall ye fear other gods. But the LORD your God ye shall fear; and he shall deliver you out of the hand of all your enemies. Howbeit they did not hearken, but they did after their former manner. So these nations feared the LORD, and served their graven images, both their children, and their children's children: as did their fathers, so do they unto this day." 2 Kings 17:37-41

Some know God's commandments, His ordinances, and laws; but they will not obey. There are many deliverance ministers and deliverance candidates, who disobey God's words outright and yet, pray, fast and demand for God's mercy. They break God's covenant and serve other gods; yet insist that God must deliver them. They pay people to pray for them, believing that God will ignore their sins and deliver them. If you disobey God outright, and yet receive your deliverance, it is not from God and it will not last.

If you come to church but refuse to repent and do all necessary restitution, yet you pray and fast for your deliverance, you are not serious. Even if you receive an answer, it is not from the Almighty God; it is from the devil and it will not last. If you really repent and identify yourself with God, He will be jealous of you and deliver you for His name's sake. If God's name is mentioned in truth and spirit in your life, He will deliver you for the sake of His name in your life.

"Make thy face to shine upon thy servant: save me for thy mercies' sake." Psalms 31:16

"Look thou upon me, and be merciful unto me, as thou usest to do unto those that love thy name." Psalms 119:132.

If you become God's property through true repentance, He can deliver and do anything for you for the sake of His name. A person that truly loves God will obtain God's mercy.

"Know therefore that the LORD thy God, he is God, the faithful God, which keepeth covenant and mercy with them that love him and keep his commandments to a thousand generations;" Deuteronomy. 7:9.

"And said, I beseech thee, O LORD God of heaven, the great and terrible God, that keepeth covenant and mercy for them that love him and observe his commandments…O Lord, I beseech thee, let now thine ear be attentive to the prayer of thy servant, and to the prayer of thy servants, who desire to fear thy name: and prosper, I pray thee, thy servant this day, and grant him mercy in the sight of this man. For I was the king's cupbearer." Nehemiah 1:5,11.

If you enter into covenant of salvation with God, your name will be written in the book of life. As long as you remain true to your relationship with God, no matter how far the devil has taken you away from your inheritance, God will have mercy on you and deliver you from every trouble for His name sake. God can do anything to protect His integrity as long as you keep His covenant with you. He is a faithful God; keeping God's covenant goes line in line with God's mercy. If you really love God with all your heart; keeping his covenant and observing His commandments, God's ears will be attentive to your prayers.

If your desire is to serve God immediately you are born again, fear Him. You will surely prosper in all that you do. God's mercy comes without hindrance when your repentance is from your heart. I want you to know that 99% of people praying for deliverance and God's mercy are not truly repented from their hearts. The answers they also receive are not from God. The devil has empowered so many deliverance ministers to transfer or postpone his activities in people's life. They pray and the devil answers while they give glory to the devil and their selves. Therefore, if you truly want God's mercy, you have to truly repent and be ready to give Him all glory for every work.

The second purpose for God's mercy is to give God glory and praise; He in turn protects His children.

"That they would desire mercies of the God of heaven concerning this secret; that Daniel and his fellows should not perish with the rest of the wise men of Babylon. Then was the secret revealed unto Daniel in a night vision. Then Daniel blessed the God of heaven. Daniel answered and said, Blessed be the name of God for ever and ever: for wisdom and might are his:" Daniel 2:18-20.

"O give thanks unto the LORD; for he is good; for his mercy endureth for ever...And with them Heman and Jeduthun, and the rest that were

chosen, who were expressed by name, to give thanks to the LORD, because his mercy endureth for ever;" 1 Chronicles. 16:34, 41.

In the absence of God's mercy, the enemy will persecute and waste God's children. They will perish with the rest of the people on earth in times of judgment and problems. When God releases His mercy, His children will be bold before others to talk about their God. At the release of God's mercy, God's children are bold in the presence of shame because their shame will be replaced with unmeasured blessings and boldness. God's mercy brings divine joy that compels even the enemies to see God's goodness. It moves men to praise and thank God. The presence of God's mercy destroys evil and forces praises out of people's mouth (2Chronicles 5:13, 14; 7:3, 6, 20-22).

God's mercy gathers people to praise God. It fills a place with divine presence and His glory. At God's mercy, His children are protected everywhere because His mercy comes with His full presence. People will see the reason to praise God, thank Him, and give all glory to Him. Without God's mercy, people will be removed from their inheritance, denied of joy, peace, and rest. Sorrows, reproaches, disgrace and shame increase in the absence of God's mercy. People's goodness and achievement become astonishment without God's mercy. All manner of problems triumph and celebrate when a person or city lacks divine mercy. The enemies blaspheme God's name when and wherever divine mercy is lacking. Forsaking God and worshipping idols removes God's mercy far away from people (Ezra 3:11; Psalms 106:1; 107:1; 109:26, 27).

When God's goodness appears, no one can withhold from thanking God, praising Him, and shouting for joy. If you want to be happy in life, praise God with all your heart, and fulfil your destiny, seek for God's mercy. It moves people to burst into tears of joy; praising God uncontrollably, and shouting with great shout in the midst of the enemies. Nobody can stop a person or cities who receive God's mercy from being happy, praising God, and shouting with great shout. At the presence of God's mercy, the devil disappears, his problems fade away, and your enemies are put to shame. God's mercy causes people to remember God, to see His goodness clearly, and to accept their faults. Everyone knows that God's mercy is above every problem when it manifests. It destroys all the works of the devil and his agents expire; giving way for people to rejoice and praise God, who alone can give perfect joy. God's mercy endures forever. His mercy does not allow affliction to return because God work is perfect (Psalms 115:1, 2; 118:1; 136:1-6).

When the mercy of God appears, even His enemies withdraw and will not seek to take His glory. The mercy of God is different from human mercy because, like the devil and his agents' mercy, it cannot endure the test of time. No power of the devil can challenge or successfully remove God's mercy because God's mercy carries the mark of heaven. Any deliverance or blessing that comes through God's mercy cannot be removed, replaced or mocked by the devil. When you believe that your deliverance or blessings can come without God or because you are wise, or prayerful, you may receive it, but you will not have the stamp of God's mercy. It is like a letter without a signature and stamp. God's mercy will make a deliverance to stay and defy satanic attack. When you are praying for God's mercy, do not base your prayer on whom you are. This is because you may not meet the condition for God's mercy. Your reason for praying for God's mercy must not be for your righteousness, sacrifices or any human efforts.

Your righteousness and sacrifices, including your seed and faith, may not be enough to attract God's mercy. Base your prayers for mercy on God's promises, His kindness, compassion, promise and Christ has accomplished work on Calvary.

"And being let go, they went to their own company, and reported all that the chief priests and elders had said unto them. And when they heard that, they lifted up their voice to God with one accord, and said, Lord, thou art God, which hast made heaven, and earth, and the sea, and all that in them is: Who by the mouth of thy servant David hast said, why did the heathen rage, and the people imagine vain things? The kings of the earth stood up, and the rulers were gathered together

against the Lord, and against his Christ. For of a truth against thy holy child Jesus, whom thou hast anointed, both Herod, and Pontius Pilate, with the Gentiles, and the people of Israel, were gathered together, for to do whatsoever thy hand and thy counsel determined before to be done. And now, Lord, behold their threatenings: and grant unto thy servants, that with all boldness they may speak thy word, by stretching forth thine hand to heal; and that signs and wonders may be done by the name of thy holy child Jesus. And when they had prayed, the place was shaken where they were assembled together; and they were all filled with the Holy Ghost, and they spake the word of God with boldness. And the multitude of them that believed were of one heart and of one soul: neither said any of them that ought of the things which he possessed was his own; but they had all things common. And with great power gave the apostles witness of the resurrection of the Lord Jesus: and great grace was upon them all. Neither was there any among them that lacked: for as many as were possessors of lands or houses sold them, and brought the prices of the things that were sold, and laid them down at the apostles' feet: and distribution was made unto every man according as he had need. And Joses, who by the apostles was surnamed Barnabas, (which is, being interpreted, the son of consolation,) a Levite, and of the country of Cyprus, having land, sold it, and brought the money, and laid it at the apostles' feet." Acts 4:23-37.

As you pray for God's mercy, remind God of His past mercies and deliverances of Israel. Appeal to God's glory, honor, and His name. Plead with Him to preserve His name in your life as he has done for the children of Israel. Remind Him of His covenants, promises, and glory. At God's mercy, judgment will be delayed or removed completely. Appeal to God for His mercy based on the principle of His justice, not to slay the righteous with the wicked.

And therefore will the LORD wait, that he may be gracious unto you, and therefore will he be exalted, that he may have mercy upon you: for the LORD is a God of judgment: blessed are all they that wait for him." Isaiah. 30:18

"And kings shall be thy nursing fathers, and their queens thy nursing mothers: they shall bow down to thee with their face toward the earth, and lick up the dust of thy feet; and thou shalt know that I am the LORD: for they shall not be ashamed that wait for me." Isaiah. 49:23.

"Thus saith the LORD; Behold, I will bring again the captivity of Jacob's tents, and have mercy on his dwelling places; and the city shall be builded upon her own heap, and the palace shall remain after the manner thereof. And out of them shall proceed thanksgiving and the voice of them that make merry: and I will multiply them, and they shall not be few; I will also glorify them, and they shall not be small." Jeremiah. 30:18-19.

"The voice of joy, and the voice of gladness, the voice of the bridegroom, and the voice of the bride, the voice of them that shall say, Praise the LORD of hosts: for the LORD is good; for his mercy endureth for ever: and of them that shall bring the sacrifice of praise into the house of the LORD. For

I will cause to return the captivity of the land, as at the first, saith the LORD." Jeremiah. 33:11

If you pray for God's mercy, He will withdraw His anger, destroy Satan's work, and be gracious unto you. He is happy when His children become humble and pray for His mercy. Even heavens, the earth, and mountains break into joy, singing, and praises, at the release of God's mercy. God's mercy brings comfort for the comfortless, and breaks all manner of bondages, to have mercy upon the afflicted. Any land or place that is devoid of God's mercy will not be established, built or celebrated. Its inhabitants will be captured by all manner of problems, and lack of all kinds of joy, peace and rests. Not everything done in such a place or by the people will bring prosperity. Such a city and people in it will never be celebrated, because there will be the lack every good thing.

God's loving kindness, goodliness, and pity, will avoid such land and her inhabitants. The reason why some people are hated or rejected and their efforts wasted; is because they lack God's mercy. The purpose of God's mercy is to replace sorrow with joy; deliver the captives; build a person; establish him; and to dethrone the wicked. A person or a city without God's mercy will become desolate, wasted under a curse, and greatly reproachful. At God's mercy, smallness is replaced with greatness.

"And it came to pass, as he went to Jerusalem, that he passed through the midst of Samaria and Galilee. And as he entered into a certain village, there met him ten men that were lepers, which stood afar off: And they lifted up their voices, and said, Jesus, Master, have mercy on us. And when he saw them, he said unto them, go shew yourselves unto the priests. And it came to pass,

that, as they went, they were cleansed. And one of them, when he saw that he was healed, turned back, and with a loud voice glorified God, and fell down on his face at his feet, giving him thanks: and he was a Samaritan. And Jesus answering said, were there not ten cleansed? But where are the nine? There are not found that returned to give glory to God, save this stranger. And he said unto him, Arise, go thy way: thy faith hath made thee whole." Luke 17:11-19

"And that he might make known the riches of his glory on the vessels of mercy, which he had afore prepared unto glory," Romans. 9:23

"And that the Gentiles might glorify God for his mercy; as it is written, for this cause I will confess

to thee among the Gentiles, and sing unto thy name." Romans.15:9

"And I thank Christ Jesus our Lord, who hath enabled me, for that he counted me faithful, putting me into the ministry; who was before a blasphemer, and a persecutor, and injurious: but I obtained mercy, because I did it ignorantly in unbelief. And the grace of our Lord was exceeding abundant with faith and love which is in Christ Jesus. This is a faithful saying, and worthy of all acceptation, that Christ Jesus came into the world to save sinners; of whom I am chief. Howbeit for this cause I obtained mercy, that in me first Jesus Christ might shew forth all longsuffering, for a pattern to them which should hereafter believe on him to life everlasting. Now unto the King eternal, immortal, invisible, the only wise God, be honor

and glory for ever and ever. Amen." 1Timothy 1:12-17.

When God enters into a life or city with His mercy, the inhabitants glorify God with loud voices; giving thanks to God and praising Him with true heart. The mercy of God carries God's riches and His glory everywhere it manifests. Even as a sinner, if you repent, you can obtain mercy so that you can join others to praise God, glorify, and thank Him with a grateful heart. If you truly repent from your sins, God will count you faithful; putting you in an office you are destined to be, and causing you to obtain mercy. If you can repent, confess your sins, and forsake them, God will cause you to obtain mercy. A person who receives God's mercy will ever honor God and glorify Him. Once you truly repent from your heart, God adopts you into His family.

"Blessed be the God and Father of our Lord Jesus Christ, which according to his abundant mercy hath begotten us again unto a lively hope by the resurrection of Jesus Christ from the dead, To an inheritance incorruptible, and undefiled, and that fadeth not away, reserved in heaven for you," 1Peter 1:3, 4

"But ye are a chosen generation, a royal priesthood, an holy nation, a peculiar people; that ye should shew forth the praises of him who hath called you out of darkness into his marvellous light: Which in time past were not a people, but are now the people of God: which had not obtained mercy, but now have obtained mercy." 1Peter 2:9, 10

An adopted person in the family of God is entitled to abundant mercy, a life of hope, an inheritance incorruptible that cannot fade away. Nevertheless, you must ask for it; you must provoke it before you can enjoy it. Believers are chosen; separated to enjoy God's mercy so that they can praise God, live in light, and overcome every life of defeats and failures.

Chapter 6

BENEFITS OF GOD'S MERCY - 1

In the absence of God's mercy, God may allow the devil, and your enemies consume you in uncompassionate destruction. He can hand victims over to forces against him, or just watch you as evil forces attack you.

"Then shalt thou say unto them, thus saith the LORD, Behold, I will fill all the inhabitants of this land, even the kings that sit upon David's throne, and the priests, and the prophets, and all the inhabitants of Jerusalem, with drunkenness. And I will dash them one against another, even the fathers and the sons together, saith the LORD: I will not pity, nor spare, nor have mercy, but destroy them. Hear ye, and give ear; be not proud: for the LORD hath spoken. Give glory to the LORD your God, before he cause darkness, and before your feet stumble upon the dark mountains, and, while ye look for light, he turn it into the shadow of death, and make it gross darkness."
Jeremiah. 13:13-16.

In the absence of God's mercy, victims will be visited, consumed and overcome by all manner of problems. Confusion, quarrels, and fighting against one another emerges in the midst of people who lack God's mercy. No matter how much you suffer, if you don't appeal for God's mercy, none will be spared. Misunderstanding between fathers and sons without pity as they destroy each other, will characterize families, cities and nations that lack divine mercy. The evidence of lack of mercy in a person life is mass destruction, wars, lies, robbery, bloody and evil use of weapons of destruction. Sudden deaths, waste of property, proudly behavior, gross darkness, and defilement of every negotiation for peace, reigns in a life, place, and nation, where there is famine of divine mercy.

"The word which came unto Jeremiah from the LORD, when king Zedekiah sent unto him Ashur the son of Melchiah, and Zephaniah the son of Maaseiah the priest, saying, Enquire, I pray thee, of the LORD for us; for Nebuchadrezzar king of

Babylon maketh war against us; if so be that the LORD will deal with us according to all his wondrous works, that he may go up from us. Then said Jeremiah unto them, thus shall ye say to Zedekiah: Thus saith the LORD God of Israel; Behold, I will turn back the weapons of war that are in your hands, wherewith ye fight against the king of Babylon, and against the Chaldeans, which besiege you without the walls, and I will assemble them into the midst of this city. And I myself will fight against you with an outstretched hand and with a strong arm, even in anger, and in fury, and in great wrath. And I will smite the inhabitants of this city, both man and beast: they shall die of a great pestilence. And afterward, saith the LORD, I will deliver Zedekiah king of Judah, and his servants, and the people, and such as are left in this city from the pestilence, from the sword, and from the famine, into the hand of Nebuchadnezzar king of Babylon, and into the hand of their enemies, and into the hand of those that seek their life: and he shall smite them with the edge of the sword; he shall not spare them, neither have pity, nor have mercy." Jeremiah 21:1-7.

When a person and a nation is void of God's mercy, an enemy greater than them will be raised in war. All manner of problems will arise to challenge their existence without pity. God will not defend, help, or fight a person, family, or people that lack divine mercy, no matter how much they suffer. A person, family, or people that lack divine mercy may have all the weapons of war to succeed; all that it takes to have victory; but God will even turn their weapons of war against them. Their brains, intelligence, certificates, and everything, will be used against them. God fights a people or a person that lacks His mercy, and causes them to make painful heart-breaking mistakes that will bring them under their enemies unto failure.

God's anger, fury, and great wrath abide in the camp of a person or people that lack divine mercy. Developed and under-developed people, nations, and persons, cannot find solution to pestilence sent against them because of the absence of God' mercy. If you lack God's mercy, God will withdraw His pity, loving kindness, and feeling of compassion; He may allow you to suffer alone without a single helper. It is a terrible thing because even drugs and the good things of the earth, put together with the best life support will fail to deliver you.

The reason why many people are not being delivered is the absence of God's mercy. Without God's mercy, every good thing of earth will be interrupted from assisting you in captivity. The power or problems holding you down in bondage may be very small; but if you lack God's mercy, your benefits, rights, entitlements, and the rest will avoid you as dung upon the face of the earth. All determined helpers will run away because if they insist on helping you, they will die in your place, and they will not be able to deliver you.

"And when thy days be fulfilled, and thou shalt sleep with thy fathers, I will set up thy seed after thee, which shall proceed out of thy bowels, and I will establish his kingdom. He shall build a house for my name, and I will stablish the throne of his kingdom forever. I will be his father, and he shall be my son. If he commits iniquity, I will chasten him with the rod of men, and with the stripes of the children of men: But my mercy shall not depart away from him, as I took it from Saul, whom I put away before thee. And thine house and thy kingdom shall be established for ever before thee:

thy throne shall be established forever." 2 Samuel 7:12-16

God's mercy makes Him not to retain His anger; without that, His anger abides and can never be removed every moment unto death and destruction. If there is anything a deliverance candidate and a suffering person need, it is God's mercy. A person who receives God's mercy may have mountainous problems, the worst foundation, a close enemy, or dozens of Goliath in the battlefield; but he will not die in their hands. No matter the type of weapons they use against you, you will live to fulfil your destiny, God's purpose for you on earth.

"For David, after he had served his own generation by the will of God, fell on sleep, and

was laid unto his fathers, and saw corruption:"
Acts 13:36

Millions of demonic spirits of death from the bottomless pit may rise against you. The whole world; all the powers of darkness in the Middle East may rise against you; but they will not prevail. No power can waste you, your investment, and your seeds, if you obtain divine mercy. Thus the best investment on earth is not money in the bank, wealth on earth, and massive structures all over the place. If you obtain mercy and retain mercy, you have wiped out tears from your unborn children's eyes because your seed shall be established without termination from the devil.

Sin, disobedience, and wickedness without true repentance may build you a throne and prosperity. However, at your peak, God will remove all that, because it lacks divine mercy. If you lose the whole earth and keep God's mercy, you have not lost anything because God's mercy can establish you forever.

"And he saith unto them, Are ye so without understanding also? Do ye not perceive, that whatsoever thing from without entereth into the man, it cannot defile him;" Mark 7:18.

"Go and proclaim these words toward the north, and say, Return, thou backsliding Israel, saith the LORD; and I will not cause mine anger to fall upon you: for I am merciful, saith the LORD, and I will not keep anger forever. Only acknowledge thine iniquity, that thou hast transgressed against the LORD thy God, and hast scattered thy ways to the strangers under every green tree, and ye have

not obeyed my voice, saith the LORD. Turn, O backsliding children, saith the LORD; for I am married unto you: and I will take you one of a city, and two of a family, and I will bring you to Zion: And I will give you pastors according to mine heart, which shall feed you with knowledge and understanding." Jeremiah. 3:12-15.

When the mercy of God enters into a person, place a nation, that person or people is/are secure even without physical or visible helpers. If you leave God, God's mercy will leave you. God's mercy is a guarantee of God's presence and its absence. As a sinner, you can only obtain God's mercy or restore it by acknowledging your sins, confessing them and forsaking them. Absence of God's mercy drives away good people and things from victims.

"Then the LORD said unto me, the prophets prophesy lies in my name: I sent them not, neither have I commanded them, neither spake unto them: they prophesy unto you a false vision and divination, and a thing of nought, and the deceit of their heart." Jeremiah. 14:14.

"And he prayed unto the LORD, and said, I pray thee, O LORD, was not this my saying, when I was yet in my country? Therefore, I fled before unto Tarshish: for I knew that thou art a gracious God, and merciful, slow to anger, and of great kindness, and repentest thee of the evil." Jonah 4:2.

A person without God's mercy falls victim to false people, fraudsters, and deceitful people everywhere. Even if God's anger or that of the devil is released against you, with God's mercy, you will be spared and delivered. True repentance can confront every enemy of your life and give you God's great kindness. God's mercy makes Him repent of the punishment He either allowed against you or destined against you

"They did not destroy the nations, concerning whom the LORD commanded them: But were mingled among the heathen, and learned their works. And they served their idols: which were a snare unto them. Yea, they sacrificed their sons and their daughters unto devils, and shed innocent blood, even the blood of their sons and of their daughters, whom they sacrificed unto the idols of Canaan: and the land was polluted with blood. Thus were they defiled with their own works, and went a whoring with their own inventions. Therefore, was the wrath of the LORD kindled

against his people, insomuch that he abhorred his own inheritance. And he gave them into the hand of the heathen; and they that hated them ruled over them. Their enemies also oppressed them, and they were brought into subjection under their hand. Many times did he deliver them; but they provoked him with their counsel, and were brought low for their iniquity. Nevertheless, he regarded their affliction, when he heard their cry: And he remembered for them his covenant, and repented according to the multitude of his mercies. He made them also to be pitied of all those that carried them captives." Psalms 106:34-46.

"And rend your heart, and not your garments, and turn unto the LORD your God: for he is gracious and merciful, slow to anger, and of great kindness, and repenteth him of the evil. Who knoweth if he will return and repent, and leave a blessing behind him; even a meat offering and a drink offering unto the LORD your God?" Joel 2:13-14.

If God commands a person, family or nation to be destroyed; but on getting there, the destroyers found God's mercy in that place or people, they will be spared. If a backslider truly repents and confronts his destroyers with God's covenant and mercies, he will be spared, delivered and set free. The only thing that can abort or slow God's anger and bring God's kindness is His mercy. No force, no matter how powerful can stop God when he is angry except divine mercy. If the devil, his agents, strongman or any deity is against you, you can stop them with God's mercy through genuine repentance. That was what Jonah did and the determined fish vomited him by force.

"So the people of Nineveh believed God, and proclaimed a fast, and put on sackcloth, from the

greatest of them even to the least of them. For word came unto the king of Nineveh, and he arose from his throne, and he laid his robe from him, and covered him with sackcloth, and sat in ashes. And he caused it to be proclaimed and published through Nineveh by the decree of the king and his nobles, saying, let neither man nor beast, herd nor flock, taste any thing: let them not feed, nor drink water: But let man and beast be covered with sackcloth, and cry mightily unto God: yea, let them turn everyone from his evil way, and from the violence that is in their hands. Who can tell if God will turn and repent, and turn away from his fierce anger that we perish not? And God saw their works that they turned from their evil way; and God repented of the evil, that he had said that he would do unto them; and he did it not." Jonah 3:5-10.

Your prayers and fasting like Jonah in the belly of the fish can do nothing against the power that has swallowed you if you are not truly born again. When God decided to overthrow the city of Nineveh after forty days, He left them only one option - repentance. Once the whole city responded and repented, the mercy of God turned away God's anger. The evil that was intended against them from God was removed, how much less any problem against you from devil.

"And God was displeased with this thing; therefore, he smote Israel. And David said unto God, I have sinned greatly, because I have done this thing: but now, I beseech thee, do away the iniquity of thy servant; for I have done very foolishly. And the LORD spake unto Gad, David's seer, saying, Go and tell David, saying, thus saith the LORD, I offer thee three things: choose thee one

of them, that I may do it unto thee. So Gad came to David, and said unto him, thus saith the LORD, choose thee Either three years' famine; or three months to be destroyed before thy foes, while that the sword of thine enemies overtaketh thee; or else three days the sword of the LORD, even the pestilence, in the land, and the angel of the LORD destroying throughout all the coasts of Israel. Now therefore advise thyself what word I shall bring again to him that sent me. And David said unto Gad, I am in a great strait: let me fall now into the hand of the LORD; for very great are his mercies: but let me not fall into the hand of man. So the LORD sent pestilence upon Israel: and there fell of Israel seventy thousand men. And God sent an angel unto Jerusalem to destroy it: and as he was destroying, the LORD beheld, and he repented him of the evil, and said to the angel that destroyed, it is enough, stay now thine hand. And the angel of the LORD stood by the threshing floor of Ornan the Jebusite." 1 Chronicles 21:7-15

"Is Ephraim my dear son? Is he a pleasant child? For since I spake against him, I do earnestly remember him still: therefore, my bowels are troubled for him; I will surely have mercy upon him, saith the LORD." Jeremiah. 31:20

"Return, O LORD, how long? and let it repent thee concerning thy servants. O satisfy us early with thy mercy; that we may rejoice and be glad all our days." Psalms 90:13-14.

If God can change His mind, and reverse His judgment because of His mercy, no other power can stand against God's mercy. When the great mercy of God manifests in any place, every problem will bow. If God can stop the angel of death, every other problem from the devil and his agents can be stopped by God's great mercy. The mercy of God is one of His promises. So if you repent and pray for God's mercy, you will receive it when. You will be satisfied with God's mercy; joy and gladness will fill your days. The reason why people's lives are filled with all manner of problems is because of lack of God's mercy. One of the benefits of God's mercy is peace, happiness and rest without distractions.

"For a small moment have I forsaken thee; but with great mercies will I gather thee. In a little wrath I hid my face from thee for a moment; but with everlasting kindness will I have mercy on thee, saith the LORD thy Redeemer." Isaiah 54:7-8

"And the sons of strangers shall build up thy walls, and their kings shall minister unto thee: for in my wrath I smote thee, but in my favor have I had mercy on thee." Isaiah 60:10

The mercy of God makes Him reverse the consequences of His anger. If God forsakes you and the enemy afflicts you, it is just for a moment if you can plead for God's mercy. The reason why many families, human organs, businesses, etc., suffer for long is because of the absence of God's mercy. Whatever you have lost - your health, peace, wealth, power, anointing - can be recovered if only you can pray for God's great mercies. God's mercy gathers ancestral and personal lost blessings together. If you are a sinner, backslider, or a believer under demonic affliction, affliction is not meant to last too long if you can repent, and forsake your sin. Both problems that come from God and the devil can be stopped if you can ask for God's mercy. Whoever can consistently follow God and keep His commandments no matter what, when God's mercy comes, it will be everlasting and unmoved, no matter the forces against him.

Whatever the devil and his agents can waste, remove or terminate, can be recovered, restored, and remain unmoved forever when God's mercy comes, if only you can stick to God's word under the situation.

"And I will not have mercy upon her children; for they be the children of whoredoms. For their mother hath played the harlot: she that conceived them hath done shamefully: for she said, I will go after my lovers, that give me my bread and my water, my wool and my flax, mine oil and my drink...And I will sow her unto me in the earth;

and I will have mercy upon her that had not obtained mercy; and I will say to them which were not my people, thou art my people; and they shall say, Thou art my God." Hosea 2:4-5-23

"Mine anger was kindled against the shepherds, and I punished the goats: for the LORD of hosts hath visited his flock the house of Judah, and hath made them as his goodly horse in the battle…And I will strengthen the house of Judah, and I will save the house of Joseph, and I will bring them again to place them; for I have mercy upon them: and they shall be as though I had not cast them off: for I am the LORD their God, and will hear them." Zechariah. 10:3, 6.

God's mercy does not stop only with the recipient, but will be extended upon his children. If the children of the recipient sin, God's mercy will be waiting for them; and as soon as they repent it will manifest. If your children refuse to repent, they will still have right to enjoy God's mercy but they will not be fit to enjoy it until they repent; it is their benefit. If you come from a family or place that lacks God's mercy, once you repent, you will be automatically connected to God's mercy.

"They shall not hunger nor thirst; neither shall the heat nor sun smite them: for he that hath mercy on them shall lead them, even by the springs of water shall he guide them." Isaiah 49:10

When God's mercy appears, the benefactors will be empowered with boldness to fight every battle and win. They will receive the strength to do exploits, move forward, and receive restorations of what they have lost. Every hunger and thirst ends because God's mercy will connect them to the springs of every good thing; they will not lack any good thing.

"Have mercy upon me, O God, according to thy loving kindness: according unto the multitude of thy tender mercies blot out my transgressions." Psalms 51:1

"O remember not against us former iniquities: let thy tender mercies speedily prevent us: for we are brought very low." Psalms 79:8.

God's mercy can wipe offences and blot out your transgressions. No matter how sinful you are; how bad and abominable you are; if you repent and pray for God's mercy, your transgressions will be blotted out. All your former iniquities; sins you are used to will be remembered no more. God's mercy arrives immediately, and speedily prevents you from all the past consequences of sins, and prevents you from former attacks. The manifestations physically may at times be delayed, but with time as you keep serving God, they will manifest.

"Remember not the sins of my youth, nor my transgressions: according to thy mercy remember thou me for thy goodness' sake, O LORD."
Psalms 25:7

"By mercy and truth iniquity is purged: and by the fear of the LORD men depart from evil."
Proverbs. 16:6

When God's mercy arrives, the foundational youthful sins will be forgotten; remembered no more; and transgressions are abolished. They will be replaced with God's goodness because of the presence attached to God's mercy. God's mercy drives iniquities far away and purges them out of their former place. It attracts God's fear and eliminates all sorts of evil from the benefactors.

"Hear me, O LORD; for thy loving kindness is good: turn unto me according to the multitude of thy tender mercies. And hide not thy face from thy servant; for I am in trouble: hear me speedily." Psalms 69:16-17.

"For a small moment have I forsaken thee; but with great mercies will I gather thee." Isaiah 54:7.

"Therefore thus saith the LORD; I am returned to Jerusalem with mercies: my house shall be built in it, saith the LORD of hosts, and a line shall be stretched forth upon Jerusalem." Zechariah. 1:16.

The mercy of God makes God turn to you or return to you. It prevails over God to hear your cries, and show you kindness with His presence. His face turns to you, with multitudes of His mercy, troubles and sorrows end with speed. When God's mercy returns, every good thing returns with it, and in a moment of time, sorrows are converted to joy and troubles to happiness. The mercy of God provides materials to restart God's abandoned projects in one's life and in a city. Difficult things are made easy and the impossible becomes possible without negotiations. It is a big minus to live without God's mercy.

"Return, O LORD, deliver my soul: oh save me for thy mercies' sake." Psalms 6:4

"For if ye turn again unto the LORD, your brethren and your children shall find compassion before them that lead them captive, so that they shall come again into this land: for the LORD your God is gracious and merciful, and will not turn away his face from you, if ye return unto him." 2 Chronicles 30:9.

"Turn thee unto me, and have mercy upon me; for I am desolate and afflicted." Psalms 25:16.

God's mercy comes with peace, salvation, and divine presence. The best way to obtain God's mercy is to seek God, turn to Him. If you do so, His mercy will manifest immediately. Doing things that please God draws his presence closer to you. A person or city that draws close to God in character and prayers will be filled with His compassion. Problems and enemies' attacks will never swallow such person or people. No power or problem can take them captive for a long time. Even their worst enemies will find reasons to help them and show them kindness. God's mercy comes with great freedom to set the captives free. The recipients of God's mercy shall be returned to their place of inheritance quickly, unless they refuse to obey God's word, and do the things that please Him. No enemy will oppress you too long if you really return to God with all your heart and keep His commandments.

Turning to God with true repentance and having a change of mind brings God mercy to take you away from affliction. No person can receive God's mercy and remain desolate, under satanic oppression forever. God's mercy comes with power and strength to deliver the captives from their captors. No captor or power can match the strength it carries. At the sight of God's mercy, every evil force bows. The hope of an enemy vanishes in vanity at the sight of God's mercy. The mightiest of evil powers are cast down when God's mercy present itself in the battlefield. No demon is so fierce and bold to dare God's mercy in the battlefield.

When God's mercy comes into a life, or place with a purpose, no force can stand against it. The only thing that can prevent God's mercy in a person's life is when such a person refuses to leave sin alone. When a sinner fully decides for God with all his heart and pleads for God's mercy, his problems become a past tense.

"And Samuel spake unto all the house of Israel, saying, if ye do return unto the LORD with all your hearts, then put away the strange gods and Ashtaroth from among you, and prepare your hearts unto the LORD, and serve him only: and he will deliver you out of the hand of the Philistines. Then the children of Israel did put away Baalim and Ashtaroth, and served the LORD only." 1 Samuel 7:3-4.

God's mercy turns God against all kinds of problems. At God's mercy, whatsoever and whosoever among the creature's bows. Why? I can answer. God's mercy comes into the battlefield with divine provision of a substitute and sin bearer; the perfect present to every enemy; the vicarious death of Christ, and redemption through His blood. This blood if well appropriated by faith cripples every evil claim over your life. So the most sinful person who repents and turns away from sin can obtain full deliverance by God's mercy.

By the sneezing of God's mercy in the battlefield, every problem flees. At the burning of God's mercy, sparks of destructive fire leap out to destroy the work of the devil. The breath of God's mercy kindles destructive coals of fire into the darkroom of your life to set you free. Strength abides in God's mercy to turn sorrows into joy before him that benefits from Him. When God's mercy is released from God's throne because of a person, cities, nations, and the mightiest are afraid. The weapons of darkness cannot hold, stand or operate at God's mercy. God's mercy sees the witchcraft powers, household wickedness as lighter than nothing, and as worse than useless. God's mercy sees iron-like curses, destructive covenants, and incurable sicknesses as rotten wood. Evil powers and combined forces of death cannot make God's mercy to withdraw from its original intention. The enemies' darts are counted as stubble before God's mercy. He laughs at the boasting of every problem put together upon the earth. Among all creatures in the whole universe, none can stop God's mercy when the victim is ready to repent, forsake sins, and live for God forever.

If your problems last after praying for God's mercy, it is because your records are being checked to prove your sincerity. It will soon be your turn if you are serious, because none can deceive God. Think about this: God is always ready to forgive you and fight for you, if you are ready to repent, confess, and forsake your sins.

"Let him that is taught in the word communicate unto him that teacheth in all good things. Be not

deceived; God is not mocked: for whatsoever a man soweth, that shall he also reap." Galatians 6:6-7.

If you are repenting, be sincere and true to God because He knows the end from the beginning. You cannot deceive Him. Decide to follow God under any situation, dead or alive. God's mercy can cause you to be satisfied with every good thing, make you glad, remove your afflictions, and all evil assigned to waste your destiny. God's mercy completes God's work, divine projects, and every good program in your life. It can bring God's glory, and extend it to your born and unborn children. When God arises with His mercy to save you, no power can stop Him. A whole family, city, or nation, can be delivered at the appearance of God's mercy. At the time of God's mercy, unmerited favors are harvested.

"If one be found slain in the land which the LORD thy God giveth thee to possess it, lying in the field, and it be not known who hath slain him: Then thy elders and thy judges shall come forth, and they shall measure unto the cities which are round about him that is slain: And it shall be, that the city which is next unto the slain man, even the elders of that city shall take an heifer, which hath not been wrought with, and which hath not drawn in the yoke; And the elders of that city shall bring down the heifer unto a rough valley, which is neither eared nor sown, and shall strike off the heifer's neck there in the valley: And the priests the sons of Levi shall come near; for them the LORD thy God hath chosen to minister unto him, and to bless in the name of the LORD; and by their word shall every controversy and every stroke be tried: And all the elders of that city, that are next unto the slain man, shall wash their hands over the

heifer that is beheaded in the valley: And they shall answer and say, Our hands have not shed this blood, neither have our eyes seen it. Be merciful, O LORD, unto thy people Israel, whom thou hast redeemed, and lay not innocent blood unto thy people of Israel's charge. And the blood shall be forgiven them. So shalt thou put away the guilt of innocent blood from among you, when thou shalt do that which is right in the sight of the LORD."
Deuteronomy. 21:1-9

God's mercy makes Him forgive the plea of the blood guilty men. If you plead for God's mercy, He will defend you from every crying blood, and vindicate you from every evil accusation.

"Two men went up into the temple to pray; the one a Pharisee, and the other a publican. The Pharisee

stood and prayed thus with himself, God, I thank thee, that I am not as other men are, extortioners, unjust, adulterers, or even as this publican. I fast twice in the week; I give tithes of all that I possess. And the publican, standing afar off, would not lift up so much as his eyes unto heaven, but smote upon his breast, saying, God be merciful to me a sinner. I tell you, this man went down to his house justified rather than the other: for every one that exalteth himself shall be abased; and he that humbleth himself shall be exalted." Luke 18:10-14.

God's mercy brings justification. Many deliverance candidates instead of pleading for God's mercy stand to claim self-righteousness. They compare themselves with others and base their deliverance on the work they do for God without humility. They are deceived to believe that once they pray aggressive judgment prayers, and fast for a period of time, their deliverance will come. They stand before God without humility and try to force God to deliver them because of the multitude of religious works they do. They are taught to sow seeds, pray hard and fast for a long time without true repentance. They forget that no one's righteousness can obtain deliverance. They forget that even the little self-righteousness they show is by God's grace, and not enough to appear before God to receive anything good. They forget what they call minor disobedience and transgression. Your best service to God without God's nature and true repentance voids your deliverance.

Every man is totally inclined to evil, and guilt; and without excuse, deserves the condemnation and judgment of a just and holy God. In one way or the other, you have broken God's law; thereby, incurring the death penalty. Every man, both sinners and saints, coming to God with his righteousness, is under deceit. If you do not come to

God with Christ's own righteousness, you will never get true and lasting deliverance. No matter your title, goodness, and works for God, they are not enough to set your deliverance. Your prayers for deliverance is not going to be answered based on your title, fasting, seed sowing, tithing, or fasting too long without the sacrifice of Christ's blood on the cross of Calvary. You must come to God in humility, trembling, and asking for His mercy.

The reasons for the prayer and fasting for our deliverance should be God's promises, and Christ's accomplished work on Calvary. You must plead for God's mercy because you may not meet the conditions for your deliverance. If you come to God like the Pharisees because you have a title - you work for God, sow seeds, fast, or do great work in the church- you may never be delivered.

"Go and proclaim these words toward the north, and say, Return, thou backsliding Israel, saith the LORD; and I will not cause mine anger to fall upon you: for I am merciful, saith the LORD, and I will not keep anger forever. Only acknowledge thine iniquity, that thou hast transgressed against the LORD thy God, and hast scattered thy ways to the strangers under every green tree, and ye have not obeyed my voice, saith the LORD." Jeremiah. 3:12-13.

"And when thy days be fulfilled, and thou shalt sleep with thy fathers, I will set up thy seed after thee, which shall proceed out of thy bowels, and I will establish his kingdom. He shall build an house for my name, and I will stablish the throne of his kingdom forever. I will be his father, and he shall

be my son. If he commit iniquity, I will chasten him with the rod of men, and with the stripes of the children of men: But my mercy shall not depart away from him, as I took it from Saul, whom I put away before thee. And thine house and thy kingdom shall be established for ever before thee: thy throne shall be established forever." 2 Samuel 7:12-16

You must appear before God for your deliverance based on His principle of justice; reminding Him of His past mercies and deliverance of His people. Lay before him His glory, honor, and preservation of His great name before the heathen. Your deliverance prayers must depend upon God's great mercy and longsuffering. Not of your work, your righteousness, or the laws you keep; it is by God's grace and mercy. If you want true deliverance, forget about your works and acknowledge your iniquity. Turn to God and fully decide to serve Him alone with all your heart. In prayers, ask for His mercy. If you obtain God's mercy, your deliverance will be perfect. Without God's mercy, everything you have is temporary and will be taken with time. Deliverance without God's mercy with time takes away all that you have and abandons you forever.

"My mercy will I keep for him for evermore, and my covenant shall stand fast with him. His seed also will I make to endure forever, and his throne as the days of heaven. If his children forsake my law, and walk not in my judgments; If they break my statutes, and keep not my commandments; Then will I visit their transgression with the rod, and their iniquity with stripes. Nevertheless, my loving kindness will I not utterly take from him, nor suffer my faithfulness to fail. My covenant will

I not break, nor alter the thing that is gone out of my lips." Psalms 89:28-34

Deliverance obtained through God's mercy attracts God's true blessings and keeps one in covenant with God. Such deliverance can endure from generation to generation. Deliverance that is void of God's mercy is unprofitable, useless and unproductive. Deliverance ministers who take money, gifts, etc., from deliverance candidates, without telling them the truth are not serving God. Deliverance ministers must confront every deliverance candidate to repent, turn away from all known sins; having a change of mind, purpose and action. They must be told to abhor and hate sin. Any deliverance candidate that wants deliverance from God is required repent, as far as it lies within their part.

"When I said, my foot slippeth; thy mercy, O LORD, held me up." Psalms 94:18.

"For the king trusteth in the LORD, and through the mercy of the most High he shall not be moved." Psalms 21:7.

You must seek for God's mercy if you want your deliverance to profit you. God's mercy makes God to confront you to repentance when you sin. No power can move you to problem at the presence of God's mercy (Luke 1:72-75; Romans. 9:15-23; 1Corinthians 7:25). God's mercy enables you to maintain your walk with God in holiness and righteousness.

"Therefore seeing we have this ministry, as we have received mercy, we faint not; But have renounced the hidden things of dishonesty, not walking in craftiness, nor handling the word of God deceitfully; but by manifestation of the truth commending ourselves to every man's conscience in the sight of God." 2 Corinthians 4:1-2

"And I thank Christ Jesus our Lord, who hath enabled me, for that he counted me faithful, putting me into the ministry; Who was before a blasphemer, and a persecutor, and injurious: but I obtained mercy, because I did it ignorantly in unbelief. And the grace of our Lord was exceeding abundant with faith and love which is in Christ Jesus." 1Timothy 1:12-14

In times of weakness, trials, and temptations, when your feet are about to clip into problems, God's mercy is made manifest to hold you. If you obtain God's mercy, it will protect you from troubles, and keep you from destructions. Those who cry unto God in times of trouble will receive answer and obtain mercy from God. To have mercy is a promise, and God is ready to perform His mercy even in the midst of troubles and demonic presence. At the manifestation of God's mercy, His covenant is remembered and performed without negotiation. God's mercy attracts direct deliverance from God that can take victims out of heavy problems and troubles.

"Be merciful unto me, O God: for man would swallow me up; he fighting daily oppresseth me."
Psalms 56:1

"And hath redeemed us from our enemies: for his mercy endureth forever." Psalms 136:24

"For the LORD will have mercy on Jacob, and will yet choose Israel, and set them in their own land: and the strangers shall be joined with them, and they shall cleave to the house of Jacob. And the people shall take them, and bring them to their place: and the house of Israel shall possess them in the land of the LORD for servants and handmaids: and they shall take them captives, whose captives they were; and they shall rule over their oppressors." Isaiah 14:1-2.

In the absence of God's mercy on earth, many powerless people will be swallowed up by wicked men. The devil brings fighting and oppression upon the helpless. God's mercy brings deliverance and redemption from stubborn enemies. In fact, stubborn and uncompromising enemies bow only at the appearance of God's mercy. Jacob, the son of Isaac, and his twin brother, Esau, faced a lot of troubles bigger than them. But Jacob lived to testify because of God's abundant mercy in his life. His life was full of weakness and sinful lifestyle. But his decisions for change brought God's mercy unto his life. Jacob, as God's choice, took place because of his decision to depend upon God for his mercy. The land of promise was given to him because of divine mercy, not by merit. When God's mercy manifests, it brings victims into rest and causes them to possess their possessions. When a person is brought into rest by God's mercy, he shall rule over his former oppressors and capture his captors. In other words, God's mercy removes oppression from its benefactors and set the captives free.

"And all his servants passed on beside him; and all the Cherethites, and all the Pelethites, and all the Gittites, six hundred men which came after him from Gath, passed on before the king. Then said the king to Ittai the Gittite, wherefore goest thou also with us? Return to thy place, and abide with the king: for thou art a stranger, and also an exile. Whereas thou camest but yesterday, should I this day make thee go up and down with us? Seeing I go whither I may, return thou, and take back thy brethren: mercy and truth be with thee." 2 Samuel 15:18-20

"Now therefore, our God, the great, the mighty, and the terrible God, who keepest covenant and mercy, let not all the trouble seem little before thee, that hath come upon us, on our kings, on our princes, and on our priests, and on our prophets, and on our fathers, and on all thy people, since the

time of the kings of Assyria unto this day. Howbeit
thou art just in all that is brought upon us; for
thou hast done right, but we have done wickedly:
Nehemiah 9:32-33.

No problem or suffering, including the enemies, survives God's mercy. His mercies deliver you from unnecessary sufferings and all manner of problems. The enemies' strength fails and they are consumed and utterly destroyed at God's mercy. No matter the strength of your problems; how big they are and the number of evil ones that rise against you; they bow at God's mercy. God's mercy brings joy in the midst of adversities and troubles. He withdraws his mercy from your enemies and disobedient children, and puts very heavy yokes on them. If you cry to Him in times of trouble and heavy yoke, He will have mercy on you. Even at the point of death, if you pray, you will obtain mercy. Nevertheless, if you do not pray for mercy, you will have sorrow upon sorrow (Psalms 9:13; Philippians 2:27-28; Psalms 31:7; Isaiah 9:17; 47:6; Matthew. 20:29-34).

God's mercy guarantees life; you will not be consumed by Him, your enemies, or your problems.

"I will praise thee with uprightness of heart, when I shall have learned thy righteous judgments."
Psalms 119:7

"It is of the LORD'S mercies that we are not consumed, because his compassions fail not. They are new every morning: great is thy faithfulness."
Lamentations. 3:22-23

His mercy brings true judgment and praise. God's mercy can keep you alive to fulfil your destiny on earth; establish your children and preserve them after your death forever. It can anoint, strengthen, and deliver you from wicked ones. Divine mercies can beat down your enemies, plague those who hate you, and keep his faithfulness with you. He will establish you beyond the sea, exalt you, and be a Father to you. God's mercy can make God the Rock of your salvation, and promote you higher than many kings. It can bring down divine presence; make you enjoy heaven on earth (2 Samuel 7:12-16 1Chronicles 17:12-15. Psalms 89: 20-29).

God's mercy can position and enable you to fight your enemies, and be victorious in life.

"But thou, O LORD, be merciful unto me, and raise me up, that I may requite them." Psalms 41:10

"Be merciful unto me, O God: for man would swallow me up; he fighting daily oppresseth me." Psalms 56:1

When God's mercy appears, you will be raised in the midst of your enemies. Without God's mercy, your enemies will finish you; consume, and fight you unto death. At His mercy, divine soldiers rise to fight your battles. The Lord will set an ambush for the enemies that will rise against you (2 Chronicles 20:21-22; Psalms 136:10-24; 143:12; Hosea. 1:7; Matthew 17:15-18).

God's mercy brings vindications and sets the captives free from every bondage (Psalms 59:10; 89:20-25; 143:12). At His mercy, every Egyptian-like problem is dealt with. Whoever stands as a hindrance is wasted at God's mercy. He can go to any extent to deliver whoever receives His mercy. His strength is manifested at His mercy to destroy the powers of your enemies. At his mercy, His hands are stretched out to take you away from the problems stronger than you do. Nothing on earth, not even nature, can prevent God from actions that can set you free at His mercy.

You can walk across the un-crossable and pass before your enemies who were determine to waste you. In fact, your enemies are your helpers in the presence of God's mercy. Natural powers give up their battle when God's children move under divine mercy. If you want victory over your enemies that are stronger than you and natural hindrances, ask God for His mercy. Once you obtain God's mercy, every wise demon withdraws from the battlefield to avoid disgrace and shame. God's mercy can stand every Pharaoh, evil blockages, organized dark kingdom; and march across demonic-determined fearful destroyers. God's mercy can stand in the midst of demonic strongholds and deliver those who obtained mercy. No matter how terrible your enemies are, they cannot confront God's mercy and live to tell the story. God's mercy endures forever in the face of charms, occult powers, and uncompromising enemies. God's mercy does not take no for an answer, or enter into negotiation with problems. God's mercy breaks every standing backbone, and frustrates heartless sadists to extinction.

If you want to be victorious in life, ask for God's mercy. If you want to prosper without pains, ask for God's mercy. If you want to be free from your enemies, ask for God's mercy. Deliverance can be hindered when you pray all manner of prayers without praying for God's mercy. Your problems may mock you, stare at your face, and waste all your effort in life, when you do not obtain divine mercy. At God's mercy, God can bring you to your Promised Land. He can prolong your life no matter the number of your enemies. At God's mercy, no evil covenant or curse can stand against you. At God's mercy, you will bear God's children. At God's mercy, all your needs can be provided. At God's mercy, God can build an ark for you to escape all kinds of problems.

I want to assure you that nothing on earth can stand to confront God's mercy. In fact, every knees bow at God's mercy. At God's mercy, every enemy of your life will be scattered. I have lived long on earth as a believer, and I can say that every problem can be solved at divine mercy. Do you know that the worst criminal or wicked person who turns to God for His mercy can be saved? Do you know that no matter how good or righteous think you are; you can die with your problem if you don't ask for God's mercy? Do you know that every sin can be forgiven if you obtain God's mercy? It does not matter how many grudges people harbor against you, if you can obtain God's mercy. No matter how old you are, if you obtain God's mercy, you can do all things. Wasted years can be restored if you obtain mercy from God. No matter how discomforting a situation you are in now, you can be comforted if you receive God's mercy. I am a living witness of divine mercy. If I die today, the mercy of God will continue in my family. WHY? - Because God's mercy endures forever.

"And when thy days be fulfilled, and thou shalt sleep with thy fathers, I will set up thy seed after thee, which shall proceed out of thy bowels, and I will establish his kingdom. He shall build an house for my name, and I will stablish the throne of his kingdom forever. I will be his father, and he shall be my son. If he commits iniquity, I will chasten him with the rod of men, and with the stripes of the

children of men: But my mercy shall not depart away from him, as I took it from Saul, whom I put away before thee. And thine house and thy kingdom shall be established for ever before thee: thy throne shall be established forever." 2 Samuel 7:12-16

If you know the truth, you will be set free. If you obtain God's mercy, God's hand will stop your enemies from reaching you. Do you know that God's mercy can stop you from committing sin, doing evil; and can prevent your enemies from attacking you? God's mercy can make you to be a prince, and break the yoke of slavery from you. It can make you to be recognized, respected and kept from the reach of your enemies. God's mercy can make people to love, help, defend and corporate with you. Let me challenge you. Can you point to me one thing that God's mercy can be afraid of? Is there any mountain or creature that can stand and say, "Who is God's mercy?" and survive? I do not know of any.

God's mercy can make the poor to be rich and keep you rich. God's mercy can take away your fears, and make your enemy fear you. God's mercy can remove your loneliness and give you a life partner, not a life enemy. It can open closed wombs, closed doors, and blocked gates. God's mercy can bless you, defend you, guide you, and rebuke all your enemies. God's mercy can reconcile you with your worst enemy; put terror upon them to fear you, and cause them to respect you. God's mercy transformed the hated Joseph; staying with him in the time of trials and temptation. God's mercy prospered him; used him to do what no other person could do in Egypt, and promoted him above all others.

God's mercy can promote you; cause your enemy to bow before you; help you to fulfil your destiny, and see all your positive dreams fulfilled. God's mercy can make you to be higher than your brethren; unite you with lost family, and use you to settle others; and give home to the homeless. God's mercy can give you the heathen for inheritance. Divine mercy can cause you to lead others to their inheritance. It can rest and exalt you even after death. God's mercy can spare your life in the midst of dying people, and bless you in the sight of your enemies. God's mercy can deliver you no matter how dry your environment is. God's mercy can water your own portion and prosper you in the midst of failures. You may be abandoned, afflicted as a widow, an orphan, fatherless or poor borrower. If you obtain God's mercy, all those things will be forgotten. You may be a murderer, and a wicked person. However, God's mercy can change your story and transform your life. Your story can be restored, and God's promise fulfilled in your life. You can inherit what rightfully belongs to you without stress if you can plead for God's mercy. Do you know that you can be guided, and controlled in all your movement by God's mercy? Try it and see.

The righteous can be saved from evil judgment if he obtains God's mercy. Nevertheless, without it, he may suffer unnecessary. God's mercy can keep your covenant with God; give you everlasting peace, and show you divine kindness. Do you know that by God's mercy, you can be brought to your city of refuge, and you will live safe, free from the enemies under divine security? Do you know that you can be freed from debt if you obtain divine mercy? Do you know that people will struggle to care for you, send you gifts and be happy to see you make it, if you obtain God's mercy?

All the story of "people hate me, want to kill me and harm me," will end if you receive God's mercy.

Fear of enemies, death, and failures, departs at God's mercy. The anger of the wicked and the dislike of your enemies are useless at God's mercy. They will not go far, who fights those under God's mercy. Curses expire, and spells bow at God's mercy. Sufferings, pains, and standing judgments against you surrender at the sight of God's mercy. All perverted judgments, evil decrees, and all kinds of disfavor flee at God's mercy. Asthma, diabetes, blood pressures, cancer, fibroids, heart diseases, sleeplessness, ulcers, and every health challenges cannot face God's mercy. No financial problems, marriage problems, satanic oppressions, child problems, academic problems, career challenges, and attitude problems, can last a second before God's mercy. Let me recommend"777" to you. It is a book entitled *"Alone with God"*. It is a book with "777" pages. Learn how to be alone with God and you will obtain God's mercy. That is the secret why a nonentity like me is becoming somebody today.

Before I deviate from my subtopic, let us come back to our question.

Chapter 7

BENEFITS OF GOD'S MERCY - 2

God's mercy shields the merciful from troubles and his seeds are blessed. (Isaiah. 57:1-2; Judges 1:22-25;

Psalms 37:26; 4:21; 18:25; 2 Timothy 1:16-18; 2 Samuel 22:26).

God's mercy ensures His blessings and multiplications (Deuteronomy 7:12-14; 13:17).

God's mercy makes Him remember your sweat and labor, to reward you (Nehemiah 13:22).

His mercy ensures your increase, settlement or establishment (Genesis. 32:10; Isaiah 14:1; 54:7-8; 60:10-22; Jeremiah 42:11-12; 30:18-22; Zechariah.1:16-17;Exodus15:13; Deuteronomy. 7:12-13; 2 Samuel 7:12-16; 1 Kings 3:6; 8:23-24; 1 Chronicles 17:12-15; 2 Chronicles 1:8-9; Ezra 7:27-28; 9:9; Nehemiah 1:11; Psalms 21:7; 31:8; 33:18-19; 41:10; 89:20-29; 74:18; 118:1-5; 136:10-25; 138:8; Proverbs. 20:28).

His mercy guarantees your prosperity (Nehemiah 1:11; Isaiah 60:10-17).

1. His mercy gives you dominion (Psalms. 89:24-29).

2. His mercy ensures your longevity (Psalms. 33:18-19; 86:13; 94:17-18; Luke 1:78-79).

3. His mercy ensures you peaceful death (Isaiah 57:1-2; 1 Chronicles. 17:11-13; 2 Samuel 7:12-15).

4. His mercy ensures your marriage (Jeremiah. 33:11; Genesis. 24:12).

5. His mercy guarantees your protection (Ezekiel. 9:9; Psalms 21:7; 59:16-17; Isaiah 49:10).

6. His mercy makes Him heal you (Psalms 41:4; 6:2; 31:9; Jeremiah. 30:17-18; Matthew 9:27-30; 15:22-280; 17:15-18; 20:29-34; Mark 10:46-52; Luke 17:11-19; Philippians 2:27; Isaiah 57:17-19).

7. His mercy terminates contempt and reproaches in your life (Psalms 57:3; 86:1-17; 115:1-2; 123:3-4;

Isaiah 47:6; 60:10-17; Jeremiah 30:17-18; Romans 9:23).

8. His mercy gives you speed (Genesis 24:12, 27).

9. When God shows you mercy, men will have mercy on you, and your captors set you free from captivity (Psalms 16:7; 106:45-46; Jeremiah 42:11-12; 2 Chronicles 30:9; Genesis 43:14; Ezra 7:27-28; 9:9; Nehemiah 1:11; Proverbs 3:34).

10. His mercy is the basis for His Fulfilling His promises (Deuteronomy 13:17; 2 Samuel 7:12-16; 1 Kings 3:6; 8:23-24; 2 Chronicles 1:8-9; 6:14-15; Psalms 77:8).

11. If God's mercy fails, His promise also fails (Psalms 138:8; Pro 3:3-4; Micah 7:18-20; Luke 1:54-56, 72-74).

12. His mercy attracts His blessings (Psalms 67:1; 2 Samuel 7:12-16; 1 Chronicles 17:12-14; Isaiah 54:10-25).

13. His mercy distinguishes you from others (Daniel 2:18; Deuteronomy 7:12-15; 1 Chronicles 17:13; 2 Samuel 7:15; Psalms 86:15-17; Hosea 1:6-7).

14. His mercy makes Him not to hide His face from you (Psalms 69:16-17; 31:16; 67:1; Isaiah 54:7-8).

15. His mercy makes Him remember you (Psalms 25:7; 136:23; Jeremiah 31:20).

16. His mercy makes Him hear your prayers (Nehemiah 9:27-28; Daniel 9:18-19; Genesis 19:18-22; Nehemiah 1:5-6, 11; Psalms 4:1; 6:2; 9:13; 27:7; 30:10; 69:13; 89:16-17; 118:1-5; Zechariah 10:6).

17. God's mercy is the instrument for deliverance:

a. Mercy brings deliverance, saviors and help (Nehemiah 9:27; Isaiah 55:3-4; Jeremiah 16:5-8).

b. Mercy guarantees His liberty; deliverance with speed (Psalms 79:8; 6:4; 31:16; 44:26; 9:13; 18:50; 31:7-9; 33:18-19; 57:3; 86:13; 94:18; 109:21; 136:10-12; 143:12; 103:4; Isaiah 54:7; Deuteronomy 32:43; 2 Chronicles 20:21-22; Ezra 9:8-9; Zechariah 10:6-12; Matthew 15:22-28; 17:15-18; Luke 1:72-74; Philippians 2:27) .

Chapter 7

HOW TO RECEIVE MERCY

You can receive God's mercy through desire, repentance and prayers.

WHAT IS REPENTANCE?

Repentance simply put, signifies and implies a turning from all known sins, change of one's mind, and change of purpose and action. Feeling sorry for sin is often associated with repentance. It must be such sorrow that will cause the repentant person to abhor or hate sin. It will lead the sinner to turn away from sin with all his heart.

"The men of Nineveh shall rise in judgment with this generation, and shall condemn it: because they repented at the preaching of Jonas; and, behold, a greater than Jonas is here." Matthew 12:41.

"But let man and beast be covered with sackcloth, and cry mightily unto God: yea, let them turn everyone from his evil way, and from the violence that is in their hands. Who can tell if God will turn and repent, and turn away from his fierce anger, that we perish not? And God saw their works, that they turned from their evil way; and God repented

of the evil, that he had said that he would do unto them; and he did it not." Jonah 3:8-10.

The shallow repentance that many so called believers display is disturbing. In the time of Christ's physical ministry on earth, he told them that shallow repentance can be condemned. The repentance of the people of Nineveh was true, deep and complete. Your repentance must imitate such repentance or you will face judgment.

"Therefore I will judge you, O house of Israel, every one according to his ways, saith the Lord GOD. Repent, and turn yourselves from all your transgressions; so iniquity shall not be your ruin." Ezekiel. 18:30

"Jesus saith unto him, I am the way, the truth, and the life: no man cometh unto the Father, but by me." John 14:6.

If you look deep into your character and find sin, your repentance is not complete, and will not be accepted by God. Before you pray for divine mercy, you need to acknowledge all your sins, repent, and forsake them. Jesus knows that with your own power, without God's help, you cannot overcome sin. That is why He wants to show you the way out, the truth that leads you to true life.

"Let the wicked forsake his way, and the unrighteous man his thoughts: and let him return unto the LORD, and he will have mercy upon him; and to our God, for he will abundantly pardon." Isaiah 55:7

"And Samuel spake unto all the house of Israel, saying, if ye do return unto the LORD with all your hearts, then put away the strange gods and Ashtaroth from among you, and prepare your hearts unto the LORD, and serve him only: and he will deliver you out of the hand of the Philistines." 1 Samuel 7:3.

If you are a wicked person, the call for repentance does not exclude you. In fact, you are number one candidate. If you are unrighteous, you will never succeed in any prayer to obtain mercy, until you repent and turn to the Lord. True repentance is an open door to divine mercy while prayer is the hand that takes you from God to man. When you desire for mercy, do not stop there; desire is just a knock. You can repent without a full heart. Any repentance that ends in only confession of sin is not with all heart. When you repent, you need to confess and forsake all confessed sin. Many people confess their sin but refuse to turn away from them. The mercy of God is waiting for you as soon as you fulfil your part. That is what Samuel told all the children of Israel.

"For they themselves shew of us what manner of entering in we had unto you, and how ye turned to God from idols to serve the living and true God;" 1Thessalonians 1:9

"But shewed first unto them of Damascus, and at Jerusalem, and throughout all the coasts of Judaea, and then to the Gentiles, that they should repent and turn to God, and do works meet for repentance." Acts 26:20

Repentance is turning away from idols to God, for the purpose of serving only Him. When you truly repent, people around you anywhere you go will notice it. You may not need to convince them because they are supposed to see it, and testify that you have repented. In fact, heaven and earth will be your witness. Repentance is a universal command of God to everyone on earth. It is the basis on which God's mercy manifests. God's command for repentance is to all men everywhere without exception (Ezekiel 18:1-4. 19-22; 33:11; Acts 17:30).

If you desire God's mercy, you will obtain it. God's mercy will not allow you to perish with people who are marked to perish. God's mercy can reveal secrets to you and cause you to bless the God of heaven. It is good to say out whatever you desire from God. Even if it is to say, "God be merciful to me for the whole day, week, month or any length of time," you will obtain mercy.

"And I commanded the Levites that they should cleanse themselves, and that they should come and keep the gates, to sanctify the Sabbath day. Remember me, O my God, concerning this also, and spare me according to the greatness of thy mercy." Nehemiah 13:22

"Hear me when I call, O God of my righteousness: thou hast enlarged me when I was in distress; have mercy upon me, and hear my prayer." Psalms 4:1

In your prayer for mercy, you have to cleanse yourself and tell God all your heart's desires. Tell God in prayer, the area of your life that needs His mercy (Daniel 2:17-19; Luke 18:3; Nehemiah 13:22; Psalms 4:1; 6:2;26:11; 59:5; 86:1-55; 25:10, 16; 27:7-9; 85:7; 123:1-3; Isaiah 30:18; Zechariah 1:12; Matthew 9:27-30; 15:22-28; 17:15-18; 20:30-34; Mark 10:46-52; Luke 18:13, 35-43; Hebrews.4:16).

HOW YOU CAN PROVOKE GOD'S MERCY

To provoke, means to arouse a feeling or action. It means to incite; to call forth; to stir up purposely. Provoking God's mercy means stir God's power to fight for you; being angry against evil powers for your sake. When you provoke God's mercy, you receive immediate attention from above. The actions of the children of Israel provoked God to anger and He appeared and defended Moses. If your tormentors rise against you, you can report them to God in prayer.

"But on the morrow all the congregation of the children of Israel murmured against Moses and against Aaron, saying, Ye have killed the people of the LORD. And it came to pass, when the congregation was gathered against Moses and against Aaron, that they looked toward the tabernacle of the congregation: and, behold, the cloud covered it, and the glory of the LORD appeared. And Moses and Aaron came before the tabernacle of the congregation. And the LORD spake unto Moses, saying, get you up from among this congregation, that I may consume them as in a moment. And they fell upon their faces. And Moses said unto Aaron, take a censer, and put fire therein from off the altar, and put on incense, and go quickly unto the congregation, and make an atonement for them: for there is wrath gone out from the LORD; the plague is begun. And Aaron took as Moses commanded, and ran into the midst of the congregation; and, behold, the plague was

begun among the people: and he put on incense, and made an atonement for the people. And he stood between the dead and the living; and the plague was stayed. Now they that died in the plague were fourteen thousand and seven hundred, beside them that died about the matter of Korah. And Aaron returned unto Moses unto the door of the tabernacle of the congregation: and the plague was stayed." Numbers. 16:41-50

When God is provoked, He can separate you from the crowd, spare your life, and consume your enemies.

"Now when he had ended all his sayings in the audience of the people, he entered into Capernaum. And a certain centurion's servant, who was dear unto him, was sick, and ready to die. And when he

heard of Jesus, he sent unto him the elders of the Jews, beseeching him that he would come and heal his servant. And when they came to Jesus, they besought him instantly, saying, that he was worthy for whom he should do this: For he loveth our nation, and he hath built us a synagogue. Then Jesus went with them. And when he was now not far from the house, the centurion sent friends to him, saying unto him, Lord, trouble not thyself: for I am not worthy that thou shouldest enter under my roof: Wherefore neither thought I myself worthy to come unto thee: but say in a word, and my servant shall be healed. For I also am a man set under authority, having under me soldiers, and I say unto one, Go, and he goeth; and to another, Come, and he cometh; and to my servant, Do this, and he doeth it. When Jesus heard these things, he marvelled at him, and turned him about, and said unto the people that followed him, I say unto you, I have not found so great faith, no, not in Israel.

And they that were sent, returning to the house, found the servant whole that had been sick." Luke 7:1-10.

The faith of the centurion provoked Jesus to action against evil forces of sickness and death. When you provoke God, sickness and death bow. If you provoke God's mercy, He can visit your household and remove your shame. Any holy action, or good deed can provoke God's mercy especially when you pray (2 Timothy 1:16-18; Luke 7:36-50; 19:1-10; Jeremiah 42:9-19; 2 Chronicles 30:6-9).

HOW TO ATTRACT GOD'S MERCY BY PRAISE

To praise is to express a favorable judgment of command. It is to glorify God. It is to worship God. It is to give God thanks with a song or using an instrument of music (2 Chronicles 5:13-14). To praise is using your mouth to talk about God's mercies; making people to know His faithfulness. It is not hiding God's loving kindness but to mention them at every opportunity. Always speak of His great goodness and loving kindness.

"And when he had consulted with the people, he appointed singers unto the LORD, and that should praise the beauty of holiness, as they went out before the army, and to say, Praise the LORD; for his mercy endureth forever." 2 Chronicles 20:21.

You can imagine God's greatness, His beauty, and holiness. Appoint a day or week to apportion time to praise God alone or in a group (Isaiah 63:7; 2 Chronicles 7:3, 6; Psalms 59:16; 101:1).

For those who are looking for deliverance only through fasting and prayer, add the prayer of mercy. This is because God's mercy brings deliverance. You can receive help when you obtain mercy.

HOW TO PRAY THE PRAYER OF MERCY FOR YOUR DELIVERANCE

Finally, before you go into prayer of mercy after true repentance, make a list of all the areas of your life where you need God's mercy. One after the other, start presenting them to God. Make all your heart desires for mercy known to God in prayers.

"And they came to Jericho: and as he went out of Jericho with his disciples and a great number of people, blind Bartimaeus, the son of Timaeus, sat by the highway side begging. And when he heard

that it was Jesus of Nazareth, he began to cry out, and say, Jesus, thou Son of David, have mercy on me. And many charged him that he should hold his peace: but he cried the more a great deal, Thou Son of David, have mercy on me. And Jesus stood still, and commanded him to be called. And they call the blind man, saying unto him, be of good comfort, rise; he calleth thee. And he, casting away his garment, rose, and came to Jesus. And Jesus answered and said unto him, what wilt thou that I should do unto thee? The blind man said unto him, Lord, that I might receive my sight. And Jesus said unto him, go thy way; thy faith hath made thee whole. And immediately he received his sight, and followed Jesus in the way." Mark 10:46-52.

Blind Bartimaeus' need for mercy was not on his finance, marriage, business, hands, or legs. It was on his eyes. The enemy of his destiny closed his eyes for many years. It may be about your health condition, finance, marriage, career, academics, children, or need of overcoming attitude problems.

Research on general deliverance has shown that personal deliverance is more effective than general deliverance. Learn how to stay alone with God and ask for His mercy. Once again, I recommend my books, entitled" Alone *with God* "and *"Forty Prayer Giants"* for specific prayers. You need God's mercy. Even during general deliverance, find time to pray specific prayers of God's mercy. The second prayer of mercy is to bind and cast out the anti-mercy demons militating against divine mercy in your life.

Chapter 8

3 DAYS DECREE FOR MERCY

DAY 1

INTRODUCTION:

Absence of God's mercy makes him consume victims in uncompassionate destruction or hand them over to the power of darkness that will do it.

The word which came unto Jeremiah from the Lord, when king Zedekiah sent unto him Pashur the son of Melchiah, and Zephaniah the son of Maaseiah the priest, saying, Inquire, I pray thee, of the Lord for us; for Nebuchadrezzar king of Babylon maketh war against us; if so be that the Lord will deal with us according to all his wondrous works, that he may go up from us.

Then said Jeremiah unto them, thus shall ye say to Zedekiah: Thus saith the Lord God of Israel; Behold, I will turn back the weapons of war that are in your hands, wherewith ye fight against the king of Babylon, and against the Chaldeans, which besiege you without the walls, and I will assemble them into the midst of this city.

And I myself will fight against you with an outstretched hand and with a strong arm, even in anger, and in fury, and in great wrath. And I will smite the inhabitants of this city, both man and beast: they shall die of a great pestilence.

And afterward, saith the Lord, I will deliver Zedekiah king of Judah, and his servants, and the people, and such as are left in this city from the pestilence, from the sword, and from the famine, into the hand of Nebuchadrezzar king of Babylon, and into the hand of their enemies, and into the hand of those that seek their life: and he shall smite them with the edge of the sword; he shall not spare them, neither have pity, nor have mercy. Jeremiah 21:1-7

PRAYER OF DECREE

Father Lord, by your mercy, turn back the weapons of war in your hand against us; and in the hands of my enemies turn it against them, in Jesus name. Let all the assembled enemies of my destiny waste themselves with their own weapons, in the name of Jesus. Arise O God in your mercy, and fight my battles, in Jesus' name.

Father Lord, let your out-stretched hands fight against my enemies, in Jesus' name. Let the strong arms of the Lord be turned against my enemies, in Jesus' name.

O Lord by your mercy, remember me for good and take me away from destruction, in the mighty name of Jesus.

Let your anger and fury, your great wrath and that of my enemies be restrained from action against me, in Jesus' name. O Lord, deliver me from every evil decision against me, and remember me by your mercy, in the mighty name of Jesus.

Jesus, take away every pestilence designed to waste my life by your mercy, in Jesus' name. My Father in Heaven, frustrate every sword and weapons of destruction provided to eliminate my life, in Jesus' name.

By your mercy O Lord, command every famine to abandon my life, and find their way into the lives of my unrepentant enemies, in the name of Jesus.

Let every stubborn and unrepentant enemy seeking my life at all cost be frustrated without mercy, in Jesus' name.

O Lord, let the sharp edge of your sword cut out the wicked without mercy, in Jesus' name.

O Lord, arise against my problems and spare them not; have neither pity, nor mercy upon them, in the name of Jesus.

And when thy days be fulfilled, and thou shalt sleep with thy fathers, I will set up thy seed after thee, which shall proceed out of thy bowels, and I will establish his kingdom. He shall build an house for my name, and I will stablish the throne of his kingdom forever.

I will be his father, and he shall be my son. If he commits iniquity, I will chasten him with the rod of men, and with the stripes of the children of men:

But my mercy shall not depart away from him, as I took it from Saul, whom I put away before thee. And thine house and thy kingdom shall be established for ever before thee: thy throne shall be established forever. 2 Samuel 7:12-16

In your mercy O Lord, take away your anger from me and return to me in peace, in Jesus name.

O Lord, let my relationship with you as Father and son be restored forever by your mercy, in Jesus' name. Lord, let not your mercy depart from me forever, in the name of Jesus.

O Lord, arise in your mercy and repent of the punishment you allowed against me.

O Lord, reverse all the curses in my life and the consequences of your anger, in Jesus' name.

Have mercy upon me and wipe out all my offenses, in Jesus' name. O Lord, blot out my transgression and return to me by your mercy, in Jesus' name.

Father Lord, forgive me all my sins and cancel all the evil records against me, in the name of Jesus.

By your mercy oh Lord, wipe away all my guilt and deliver me from oppressions, in Jesus' name.

Lord, let your mercy bring into my life justification, in Jesus' name. Lord, confront and conquer all my problems, and enable me to maintain a holy life, and holy walk with you in righteousness, in Jesus' name.

Lord, by your mercy, deliver me from every unnecessary suffering, in the name of Jesus.

Father Lord, let your mercy position me and empower me to fight all my enemies, in the name of Jesus.

But thou, O Lord, be merciful unto me, and raise me up, that I may requite them.   Psalms 41:10

Be merciful unto me, O God: for man would swallow me up, he fighting daily oppresseth me. Psalms 56:1

Heavenly Father, by your mercy, bring vindication into my life, in the name of Jesus. Hear my prayers Lord, and hide not your face from me, in the name of Jesus.

Lord, let your mercy distinguish me from others and attract me blessings, in the name of Jesus.

Let your mercy bring all your promises to fulfilment into my life, in Jesus' name. O Lord my God, show me mercy and cause others to show me mercy, in Jesu's name.

In the name of Jesus, command my captors to release me and terminate my contempt forever.

Lord, protect me by your mercy; give me long life; power to prosper, and increase me in every good thing, in the name of Jesus.

DAY 2

INTRODUCTION:

God's mercies make Him not to retain His anger; causes Him to repent of the punishment He either allowed against you, destined against you, or to remove the consequences of His anger against you.

And he prayed unto the Lord, and said, I pray thee, O Lord, was not this my saying, when I was yet in my country? Therefore, I fled before unto Tarshish: for I knew that thou art a gracious God, and merciful, slow to anger, and of great kindness, and repentest thee of the evil.

And should not I spare Nineveh, that great city, wherein are more than six score thousand persons that cannot discern between their right hand and their left hand; and also much cattle? Jonah 4:2, 11

PRAYER OF DECREE:

Lord Jesus, by your mercy, slowdown your anger against me, and visit me with your great kindness, in the mighty name of Jesus. O Lord, spare my life from destruction and wipe out all my offenses against you, in Jesus name.

Merciful Father, have mercy upon me, remember my labor, and reward me, in Jesus' name.

And I commanded the Levites that they should cleanse themselves, and that they should come and keep the gates, to sanctify the Sabbath day. Remember me, O my God, concerning this also, and spare me according to the greatness of thy mercy. Nehemiah 13:22

Let your mercy O Lord, bring blessings into my life, ensure the multiplication of your goodness, and shield me from every trouble, in the name of Jesus.

Lord, by your mercy, guarantee my prosperity, dominion over my enemies, and peaceful life, in the mighty name of Jesus.

O Lord, release your lovingkindness, pity, and compassion upon my life in Jesus name.

Father, let your deep tender mercy, feelings, and compassion manifest in my life forever, in the name of Jesus.

Father Lord, be aroused by your sight of my weakness and suffering, and help me out of the captivity of the wicked in Jesus name.

Father, consider my situation and favor me today in Jesus name.

By your mercy O Lord, get involved in my life and without protocol, break every standing law and help me out of every trouble, in the name of Jesus.

When Jesus had lifted up himself, and saw none but the woman, he said unto her, Woman, where are those thine accusers? hath no man condemned thee? She said, No man, Lord. And Jesus said unto her, neither do I condemn thee: go, and sin no more. John 8:10-11

Lord Jesus, let all those who accuse me, condemn me, and wish to kill me be confronted by your mercy, in the mighty name of Jesus.

O Lord, cause all your promises to be fulfilled in my life by your mercy, in Jesus' name.

Lord, behold my weakness, suffering, and oppression, and deliver me from my captors, in the name of Jesus.

My Father, by your mercy, take away my reproach, shame, and disgrace, in Jesus' name.

By your mercy O Lord, break every evil covenant in my life, and cause my curses to expire, in the name of Jesus.

Let the blood of Jesus speak mercy into my life by force, in Jesus' name.

Oh Lord, let your mercy attract divine liberty into my life, in Jesus' name.

Father Lord, release saviors into my life. Command helpers to help me at all cost, in Jesus' name.

Therefore, thou deliveredst them into the hand of their enemies, who vexed them: and in the time of their trouble, when they cried unto thee, thou heardest them from heaven; and according to thy manifold mercies thou gavest them saviors, who saved them out of the hand of their enemies.
Nehemiah 9:27

Incline your ear, and come unto me: hear, and your soul shall live; and I will make an everlasting covenant with you, even the sure mercies of David. Behold, I have given him for a witness to the people, a leader and commander to the people.
Isaiah 55:3, 4

O Lord, command true life, abundant life, and peace to enter every organ in my body, in Jesus' name.

Lord, let me live again by your sure mercies, in the name of Jesus. Father, give me deliverance with speed and cast me not away forever, in the name of Jesus.

O Lord, let the power in your mercy destroy every demonic plan, purposes, and designs against me, in Jesus' name.

Father Lord, break the yoke of every medical negative report, rules, or laws, and set me free in Jesus name.

And, behold, a woman of Canaan came out of the same coasts, and cried unto him, saying, have mercy on me, O Lord, thou Son of David; my daughter is grievously vexed with a devil. But he answered her not a word. And his disciples came and besought him, saying, Send her away; for she crieth after us.

But he answered and said, I am not sent but unto the lost sheep of the house of Israel. Then came she and worshipped him, saying, Lord, help me.

But he answered and said, it is not meet to take the children's bread, and to cast it to dogs. And she said, Truth, Lord: yet the dogs eat of the crumbs which fall from their masters' table.

Then Jesus answered and said unto her, O woman, great is thy faith: be it unto thee even as thou wilt. And her daughter was made whole from that very hour. Matthew 15:22-28

Heavenly Father, ignore my past mistakes and wickedness, and accept my repentance by your mercies, in Jesus' name.

Oh Lord, Respect not every evil sacrifice, negative utterances, and confront my problems unto death, in Jesus' name.

Lord, let every word against my deliverance be pushed away by your mercy, in the name of Jesus.

For your name's sake oh Lord, have mercy upon me and protect your integrity in my life, in Jesus' name

O God, let my condition, repentance, prayers, and praise provoke your mercy into my life in Jesus' name.

Father, let your presence manifest in my situation for immediate deliverance, in the name of Jesus. Lord of glory, by your mercy, let my eagle fly again in power in Jesus name.

DAY 3

INTRODUCTION:

God's mercy removes oppression; destroys sufferings, solves problems and gives long life.

Hear, O Lord, when I cry with my voice: have mercy also upon me, and answer me. Psalms 27:7

Behold, the eye of the Lord is upon them that fear him, upon them that hope in his mercy; To deliver their soul from death, and to keep them alive in famine. Psalms 33:18, 19

PRAYER OF DECREE:

As I cry today unto my God in prayer and fast, let God's mercy bring answers to me, in Jesus' name.

Father Lord, by your mercy, deliver me from every trouble and death; and keep me alive by your mercy, in the name of Jesus.

Every embargo placed upon my life by the wicked, be lifted by divine mercy, in the name of Jesus (Psalms 67:1. Isaiah 54:10-25)

Let God's mercy bring into my bosom every type of blessing, goodness, and fulfilment of God's promises, in the mighty name of Jesus.

Any power that is blocking God's mercy from my life, be removed by force, in Jesus' name.

I command every spirit that is expanding my problems to bow and disappear from the battlefield, in Jesus' name.

Any power blocking my progress, be destroyed by divine mercy, in Jesus' name. Every program of star hijackers in my life, be destroyed by divine mercy, in Jesus' name.

Every determined destiny killer in my life, be wasted by divine mercy, in the mighty name of Jesus.

Father Lord, by your divine mercy, ensure my increase, settlement, and establishment in your will today in my life, in Jesus' name.

I am not worthy of the least of all the mercies, and of all the truth, which thou hast shewed unto thy servant; for with my staff I passed over this Jordan; and now I am become two bands.
Genesis 32:10

For a small moment have I forsaken thee; but with great mercies will I gather thee. In a little wrath I hid my face from thee for a moment; but with everlasting kindness will I have mercy on thee, saith the Lord thy Redeemer. Isaiah 54:7, 8

By your mercy, blind every evil eye against me, destroy every head manipulator, poverty activators, evil marks, evil observers, and witchcraft's handwriting against my life, in the name of Jesus.

Father Lord, as I close my fast today, release your lovingkindness, peace, and compassion into my life, in Jesus' name.

O Lord, destroy every weakness in my life, and empower my eagle to fly by force, in the name of Jesus.

By your mercy O Lord, break every evil covenant in my life; frustrate every dark agent, and remove every evil bullet in my life, in Jesus' name.

Let my fasting end every negative power in my life, waste the powers that have arrested my destiny, and release me from every evil arrest, in the name of Jesus.

Lord Jesus, by your mercy, get involved in my life and deliver me from every confusion, evil deposits, satanic poisons, arrows of fruitless efforts, rags of poverty, evil reinforcements, occult arrows, and late progress, in the mighty name of Jesus.

Mercy of God, deliver me from every sin, enemies, troubles and every problem, in Jesus' name.

Father Lord, empower me by your mercies to be free from curses of the land.

Hear the word of the Lord, ye children of Israel: for the Lord hath a controversy with the inhabitants of the land, because there is no truth, nor mercy, nor knowledge of God in the land. By swearing, and lying, and killing, and stealing, and committing adultery, they break out, and blood toucheth blood.

Therefore, shall the land mourn, and every one that dwelleth therein shall languish, with the beasts of the field, and with the fowls of heaven; yea, the fishes of the sea also shall be taken away.
Hosea 4:1-3

Let every enemy of my progress face God's wrath and fear of day and nights by the mercies of God, in Jesus' name.

By divine mercy, I command divine whirlwind to carry away all my problems today, shock the brain of my unrepentant enemies, and hit their power with brimstone, in the name of Jesus.

Let the mercy of God contend for my greatness in the hands of my enemies, in Jesus' name.

Let the mercy of God destroy every roundabout spirit in my life; spirit of poor finishing, coffin spirit, and rain of afflictions, in Jesus' name.

As I end my fast today, I plead for God's mercy to deliver me from iron-like curses, killers of good things, unprofitable words, shame distributors, and hidden oppressors, in Jesus' name.

By the mercy of God, I terminate every problem in my life today, in Jesus' name. AMEN!

7 DAYS PRAYERS

FOR DIVINE

MERCY

Day 1

MERCY OF GOD TO TURN AWAY GOD'S ANGER

[2 Samuel 7:12-16; 14:14; Mark 7:18; Jeremiah 3:12-15]

1. Father Lord, thank you for the provision of your mercy in my life, in Jesus' name.

2. Lord, command your mercy to appear in my life by fire, in Jesus' name.

3. By the mercy of God, let my life be established, in Jesus' name.

4. Everlasting God, empower me with everlasting mercy, in Jesus' name.

5. Let the mercy of God drive away any pollution in my life, in Jesus' name.

6. Let the anger of God over my life disappear by divine mercy, in Jesus' name.

7. I command the mercy of God to fall upon me now, in Jesus' name.

8. Lord, arise and remove your anger from my foundation, in Jesus' name.

9. Father Lord, remember your covenant of mercy upon my life, in Jesus' name.

10. Mercy of God, bring me back to my divine inheritance, in Jesus' name.

11. Any power keeping me out of divine mercy; be wasted, in Jesus' name.

12. By the arrows of divine mercy, I reverse God's judgment over my life, in Jesus' name.

13. Lord, by your mercy, remove every curse you placed upon me, in Jesus' name.

14. Every problem in my life, die by divine mercy, in Jesus' name.

15. You agent of divine mercy, release God's mercy into my life, in Jesus' name.

16. Lord Jesus, have mercy upon me now, in Jesus' name.

17. Angels of the Living God, minister divine mercy into my life, in Jesus' name.

18. Any power blocking God's mercy away from me, be removed, in Jesus' name.

19. Blood of Jesus, speak divine mercy into my life today, in Jesus' name.

20. Any satanic program against God's mercy upon my life, to be terminated, in Jesus' name.

21. Father Lord, discharge your mercy into my life, in Jesus' name.

22. Every enemy of divine mercy in my life, be burnt to ashes by the Holy Ghost fire, in Jesus' name.

23. Every door of divine mercy closed against my life; open, in Jesus' name.

24. The Mercy of God that cannot be stopped, enter into my life by force, in Jesus' name.

25. Mercy of God, stop every satanic activity in my life, in Jesus' name.

MERCY OF GOD, DESTROY JUDGMENT AGAINST ME

[Psalms 106:34-46; 90:13-14; Joel 2:13-14]

1. Every judgment, hanging upon me; be removed by divine mercy, in Jesus' name.

2. Divine mercy; convince God to repent of His punishment against me, in Jesus' name.

3. Every problem destined to waste my life; be reversed by divine mercy, in Jesus' name.

4. Every satanic arrow fired against me; be reversed by divine mercy, in Jesus' name.

5. Any problem fired to destroy me; be removed by God's mercy, in Jesus' name.

6. Lord Jesus, reverse every judgment against me by your mercy, in Jesus' name.

7. Blood of Jesus, speak me out of every judgment by your mercy, in Jesus' name.

8. Every enemy of the peace of God in my life, die by divine mercy, in Jesus' name.

9. I break the strength of satanic judgment in my life by divine mercy, in Jesus' name.

10. Lord, arise and empty my life of every judgment by your mercy, in Jesus' name.

11. Let the presence of God's mercy in my life deliver me, in Jesus' name.

12. Divine mercy, confront and conquer every problem in my life, in Jesus' name.

13. Divine mercy; restore every good thing I have lost in life, in Jesus' name.

14. Father Lord, use your mercy to deliver me from every trouble, in Jesus' name.

15. Let the power in divine mercy remove every pain in my life, in Jesus' name.

Day 3

MERCY TO REVERSE EVIL CONSEQUENCES

[Isaiah 54:7-8; 60:10; Hosea 2:4-5, 23; Zechariah 10:36; Isaiah 49:10]

1. I command every evil consequence of my life to be reversed by divine mercy, in Jesus' name.

2. Any problem in my life because of my mistakes; die by divine mercy, in Jesus' name.

3. Let the consequences of my sins be removed by God's mercy, in Jesus' name.

4. I command the consequences of my idolatry to die by divine mercy, in Jesus name.

5. Any blood sacrifice, crying against me; be silenced by divine mercy, in Jesus' name.

6. Let the blood of abortion crying against me be silenced by divine mercy, in Jesus' name.

7. Every evil force, speaking evil into my life; be terminated by divine mercy, in Jesus' name.

8. Father Lord, by your divine mercy, remove your wrath from me, in Jesus' name.

9. Deposited presence of God in my life, come back by divine mercy, in Jesus' name.

10. Divine mercy; take me away from the hands of my enemies, in Jesus' name.

11. Any evil rule over my life; be terminated by divine mercy, in Jesus' name.

12. Any problem in my life; die by divine mercy, in Jesus' name.

13. Fire of God, burn to ashes every enemy of divine mercy in my life, in Jesus' name.

14. Divine mercy; chase away every attacker of my destiny, in Jesus' name.

15. Any mountain, standing against my life; be removed by divine mercy, in Jesus' name.

MERCY OF GOD, BLOT OUT MY TRANSGRESSION

[Psalms 51:1; 79:8; Habakkuk. 8:12; Psalms 25:7; Proverbs. 16:16; Mark 7:18-19]

1. Blood of Jesus, command divine mercy to manifest in my life, in Jesus' name.

2. Every sin in my life; be conquered by divine mercy, in Jesus' name.

3. Every determined enemy of my life; be defeated by divine mercy, in Jesus' name.

4. Every yoke of sin in my life; break by divine mercy, in Jesus' name.

5. Divine mercy of God; reverse every spirit of sin in my life, in Jesus' name.

6. Let the root of sin in my life be uprooted by divine mercy, in Jesus' name.

7. Every offense standing against me; disappear by divine mercy, in Jesus' name.

8. Let all accusers of my life be silenced by divine mercy, in Jesus' name.

9. Agent of transgression in my life; be disgraced by force, in Jesus' name.

10. Let the mercy of God arise, and take away every transgression in my life, in Jesus' name.

11. Powers behind all my transgressions; be wasted by divine mercy, in Jesus' name.

12. Any transgression crying against me; be frustrated by divine mercy, in Jesus' name.

13. Lord Jesus, walk me into your power of mercy, in Jesus name.

14. Every problem that came into my life by sin; be removed by divine mercy, in Jesus' name.

15. Divine mercy; take over every area of my life, in Jesus' name.

16. Every door of transgression in my life; be closed by divine mercy, in Jesus' name.

Day 5

MERCY TO RETURN GOD BACK TO ME

[Psalms 69:16-17; Isaiah 54:7; Zechariah 1:16; Psalms 6:4]

1. Mercy of God, arise and bring back God to my life, in Jesus' name.

2. Let the lovingkindness of God bring back every good thing I have lost, in Jesus' name.

3. O God, by your mercy, turn your face back to me, in Jesus' name.

4. Every messenger of trouble in my life; be removed by divine mercy, in Jesus' name.

5. Let my broken life be gathered back together by divine mercy, in Jesus' name.

6. Father Lord, return back to me with your divine mercies, in Jesus' name.

7. Wind of divine mercy; bring back divine presence into my life, in Jesus' name.

8. Fire of God, burn anything in me against divine mercy, in Jesus' name.

9. Any demon in my life working against divine mercy, I cast you out, in Jesus' name.

10. Any Goliath standing between me and divine mercy, fall down and die, in Jesus' name.

11. Pillars of witchcraft standing against God's mercy in my life; be dismantled, in Jesus' name.

12. Let the voice of divine mercy be heard in my life, in Jesus' name.

13. Any power fighting God's mercy in my life; die, in Jesus' name.

14. Blood of Jesus, take away every enemy of divine presence, in Jesus' name.

15. Every voice of the wicked crying against divine mercy in my life; shut up forever, in Jesus' name.

Day 6

MERCY OF GOD, DESTROY MY SINS

[Deuteronomy 21:6-9]

1. Let the mercy of God destroy my Adamic nature in me, in Jesus' name.

2. Let the root of sin in my life be aborted by divine mercy, in Jesus' name.

3. Every enemy of righteousness in my life; be destroyed by divine mercy, in Jesus' name.

4. O Lord, arise and release your mercy into my root, in Jesus' name.

5. I command messengers of iniquity in my life to die with their message, in Jesus' name.

6. Blood of Jesus, flow into my life and release your mercy, in Jesus' name.

7. Every demonic bondage in my life; break by divine mercy, in Jesus' name.

8. I move the power of sin out of my life by divine mercy, in Jesus' name.

9. Holy Ghost fire mingled with divine mercy; destroy sin in my life, in Jesus' name.

10. Mercy of God, cleanse my mind of every sin, in Jesus' name.

11. O hand of God, release your mercy into my inner man, in Jesus' name.

12. I stand against sin in my life by divine mercy, in Jesus' name.

13. Let the mercy of God take over my thoughts and imaginations, in Jesus' name.

14. I bind and cast out every spirit of sin in my life by divine mercy, in Jesus' name.

15. I reject every work of the devil in my life by divine mercy, in Jesus' name.

Day 7

JUSTIFICATION BY DIVINE MERCY

[Jeremiah 3:12-13; Luke 18:10-14; Psalms 89:28-34]

1. God of mercy, prosper me in righteousness, in Jesus' name.

2. Father Lord, thank you for having mercy upon me, in Jesus' name.

3. Every yoke of iniquity in my life; be broken by divine mercy, in Jesus' name.

4. O Lord, keep me under your covenant by divine mercy, in Jesus' name.

5. Every enemy of my relationship with God; die by divine mercy, in Jesus' name.

6. Let my handwork be blessed by divine mercy, in Jesus' name.

7. O Lord, by your mercy reign and rule over my life, in Jesus' name.

8. Let the lovingkindness of God prosper in my life forever, in Jesus' name.

9. Every ancestral covenant in my life; break by divine mercy, in Jesus' name.

10. Every throne of sin in my life; be destroyed by divine mercy, in Jesus' name.

11. O Lord, blot out my transgressions by divine mercy, in Jesus name.

12. Let my conscience be purged by divine mercy, in Jesus' name.

13. Mercy of God, preserve my covenant with God forever, in Jesus' name.

14. Mercy of God, empower me to live a holy life, in Jesus' name.

15. Every evil utterance ever uttered against my life; expire by divine mercy, in Jesus' name.

16. I command every work of Satan in my life to expire, in Jesus' name.

17. Let the root of sin in my life be uprooted by divine mercy, in Jesus' name.

3 DAYS PRAYERS FOR DIVINE MERCY

Day 1

MERCY OF GOD, EMPOWER ME TO WALK WITH GOD

[Psalms 94:18; Luke 1:72-75]

1. I receive power to walk with God all the days of my life, in Jesus' name.

2. Mercy of God, hold my feet to walk with God without slipping, in Jesus' name.

3. Any power that wants to move me away from God; die, in Jesus' name.

4. Blood of Jesus, increase divine mercy in my life to do good, in Jesus' name.

5. Every wicked movement against my walk with God; be terminated, in Jesus' name.

6. Mercy of God to trust God to the end; possess me, in Jesus' name.

7. Let the mercy of God save me from all my enemies, in Jesus' name.

8. Every power assigned to take me away from God's kindness; die, in Jesus' name.

9. Father Lord, multiply your goodness in my life, in Jesus' name.

10. I receive anointing to remain under divine mercy, in Jesus' name.

11. Any power pushing me to break my covenant with God; be frustrated, in Jesus' name.

12. O Lord, deliver me from every grip of sin and iniquity forever, in Jesus' name.

13. Every enemy of God's mercy in my life; be disorganized, in Jesus' name.

14. Father Lord, by your mercy; help me to serve you with fear, in Jesus' name.

15. Anointing to serve God in holiness; possess me, in Jesus' name.

16. Every root of unrighteousness in my life; be uprooted, in Jesus' name.

17. Mercy of God, promote my closeness with heaven, in Jesus' name.

MERCY OF GOD, REMOVE ME FROM OPPRESSION.

[Psalms 56:1; 136:24; Isaiah 14:1-2]

1. O Lord, thank you for your readiness to deliver me from every oppressor, in Jesus' name.

2. Any problem that has swallowed my life; vomit it by divine mercy, in Jesus' name.

3. Any battle going on against my life; be terminated by divine mercy, in Jesus' name.

4. O Lord, arise and stop every demonic oppression in my life by your mercy, in Jesus' name.

5. Every arrow of the wicked in my life; be removed by divine mercy, in Jesus' name.

6. Let the fears of my oppressors' backfir
   in Jesus' name.

7. Every enemy of my redemption; be frustrated by
   divine mercy, in Jesus' name.

8. Let the mercy of God secure my freedom by
   force, in Jesus' name.

9. Any oppressor, sitting upon my destiny; be
   unseated by divine mercy, in Jesus' name.

10. O God of mercy; stop every oppression in my
    life, in Jesus' name.

11. Every area of my life that needs divine mercy;
    receive it now, in Jesus' name.

12. O Lord, arise and single me out for your
    goodness, in Jesus' name.

13. By the mercy of God, I receive unmerited favor,
    in Jesus' name.

14. O Lord, take me to my inheritance by your mercy, in Jesus' name.

15. Any strange attack on my life; be terminated by divine mercy, in Jesus' name.

16. Any problem that has joined me this year; die by divine mercy, in Jesus' name.

17. Any evil force on assignment in my life; be disorganized, in Jesus' name.

18. Father Lord, empower me to possess my possessions, in Jesus' name.

Day 3

MERCY OF GOD, DELIVER ME FROM SUFFERING

[2 Samuel 15:18-20; Nehemiah 9:32-33; Psalms 9:13; Nehemiah 13:22; Psalms 31:7; Isaiah 9:17; 47:6; Matthew 20:21-34]

1. Every yoke of suffering in my life; break by divine mercy, in Jesus' name.

2. Mercy of God, deliver me from all manner of suffering, in Jesus' name.

3. Mercy of God, command every kind of problem to avoid me, in Jesus' name.

4. Every strange sickness in my life; die by force, in Jesus' name.

5. Any war assigned to terminate my life; I reject you by force, in Jesus' name.

6. Let the mercy of God deliver me from every hardship, in Jesus' name.

7. O Lord, release your mercy into my life for deliverance, in Jesus' name.

8. Let the almightiness of God break me loose from suffering, in Jesus' name.

9. O Lord, appear in my life with all your terribleness against my suffering, in Jesus' name.

10. Every trouble that has swallowed me, vomit me by force, in Jesus' name.

11. Any problem sitting as king or queen in my life; be overthrown, in Jesus' name.

12. Let the reign of the wicked in my life be terminated, in Jesus' name.

13. Father, by your mercy; remove the problems you brought into my life, in Jesus' name.

14. Every problem I brought into my life; die by divine mercy, in Jesus' name.

15. Any suffering that has right over my life; die by divine mercy, in Jesus' name.

16. Mercy of God, command everlasting joy and peace into my life, in Jesus' name.

17. O Lord, arise and give me rest round about, in Jesus' name.

7 Days Fast

Day 1

MERCY OF GOD, DELIVER ME FROM EVIL WASTERS

[Psalms 89:20-29; 119:7; Lamentations 3:22-23]

1. Every messenger of evil report in my life; carry your message to your sender, in Jesus' name.

2. Any waster assigned to waste my life; be wasted by divine mercy, in Jesus' name.

3. O Lord, perfect your peace in my life, in Jesus' name.

4. Every evil force that has occupied my heart; be cast out, in Jesus' name.

5. O Lord, arise and judge every evil in my habitation, in Jesus' name.

6. Any power assigned to consume me; die by divine mercy, in Jesus name.

7. Let the compassion of God surround me, in Jesus' name.

8. Every determined enemy working against my destiny; be frustrated, in Jesus' name.

9. O Lord, renew your mercy every day in my life, in Jesus' name.

10. Every good thing that has expired in my life; receive divine renewal, in Jesus' name.

11. O Lord, pour your oil of mercy upon me, in Jesus' name.

12. Mercy of God, establish me in God's will, in Jesus' name.

13. Divine mercy, command your strength into my life, in Jesus' name.

14. Every wicked plot against my life; fail woefully, in Jesus' name.

15. Mercy of God, beat down every foe around me, in Jesus' name.

16. Let all my plagues be destroyed by divine mercy, in Jesus' name.

17. Every arrow of hatred fired against my life; return to sender, in Jesus' name.

18. God's faithfulness and mercy; begin to manifest in my life, in Jesus' name.

19. Any problem that has exalted itself against God in my life; die, in Jesus' name.

20. Father Lord, remove every evil from my life, in Jesus' name.

DAY 2

MERCY OF GOD, POSITION ME TO FIGHT

[Psalms 41:10; 56:1]

1. Mercy of God, position me to win every battle, in Jesus' name.

2. I hide myself under the umbrella of divine mercy, in Jesus' name.

3. Let the mercy of God expose all my unrepentant enemies unto death, in Jesus' name.

4. Let the weapons of my enemy's backfire by fire, in Jesus' name.

5. Every evil seed in my life; die by divine mercy, in Jesus' name.

6. Every weapon against God's goodness in my life; become blunt, in Jesus' name.

7. Let the mercy of God promote me above my adversaries, in Jesus' name.

8. I command the unmerited favor of God to manifest in my life, in Jesus' name.

9. Let the oppressing power of God oppress my oppressors, in Jesus' name.

10. I stand upon the Rock to fight all my battles, in Jesus' name.

11. Blood of Jesus, speak me out of every trouble, in Jesus' name.

12. In the mighty name of Jesus, I overcome all my enemies.

13. Every organized battle against me; be disorganized by divine mercy, in Jesus' name.

14. Almighty God, command your mercies to preserve me, in Jesus' name.

15. Father Lord, take me to my right position in life, in Jesus' name.

16. Blood of Jesus, speak me out of every wrong positioning, in Jesus' name.

17. Anointing to stand with God, fall upon me, in Jesus' name.

18. Mercy of God, promote my promotion by force, in Jesus' name.

MERCY OF GOD, FIGHT FOR ME

[Hosea. 1:7; 2 Chronicles 20:21-22; Psalms 136:10-24; 143:12].

1. Any battle going on against me must end in my favor, in Jesus' name.

2. I command the morning to favor me to the end, in Jesus' name.

3. Mercy of God, fight every agent of Satan assigned to waste me, in Jesus' name.

4. Let every determined enemy of my life be confronted by God, in Jesus' name.

5. Every weapon designed to waste me; waste your owners, in Jesus' name.

6. Let my enemies fall into the pit they dug for me, in Jesus' name.

7. O Lord, as I start singing now, arise, and fight my battles, in Jesus' name.

[Begin to sing all manner of songs of warfare. Praise God with all your heart, in Jesus' name].

8. I command my enemies to use their weapons against each other, in Jesus' name.

9. Let confusion overtake my enemies wherever they are, in Jesus' name.

10. Let the brain of every determined enemy fail them, in Jesus' name.

11. Let God's anger from above frustrate every unrepentant enemy, in Jesus' name.

12. Holy Ghost, fight my battles, in Jesus' name.

13. Let the armies from heaven descend upon my stubborn enemies, in Jesus' name.

MERCY OF GOD, VINDICATE ME

[Psalms 59:10; 89:20-25; 143:12]

1. Let the plans of my enemy against me be reversed, in Jesus' name.

2. Father Lord, prevent my enemies from rejoicing over me, in Jesus' name.

3. Let the God of mercy vindicate me before my enemies, in Jesus' name.

4. I command the desires of my enemies over me to be reversed, in Jesus' name.

5. O Lord, disappoint all my enemies, in Jesus' name.

6. Let the anointing of God upon me disappoint my enemies, in Jesus' name.

7. Father Lord, prove my enemies wrong, in Jesus' name.

8. Almighty God, arise and establish me in the presence of my mockers, in Jesus' name.

9. Let the strength of God take me away from shame, in Jesus' name.

10. Every arrow of lack, fired against me; backfire, in Jesus' name.

11. Every affliction channeled against me; be diverted, in Jesus' name.

12. O Lord, arise and show me your faithfulness, in Jesus' name.

13. Let my promotion intimidate my enemies, in Jesus' name.

14. I cut myself off from every weapon of my enemies, in Jesus' name.

15. I command the destroyers of my life to be destroyed, in Jesus' name.

16. Any servant of the devil that has vowed to waste me; fail woefully, in Jesus' name.

17. Every dream of defeat prepared against me; backfire, in Jesus' name.

18. Every enemy in the battlefield against my life; be disgraced, in Jesus' name.

MERCY OF GOD, HEAR MY PRAYERS

[Nehemiah 9:27-28; Psalms 89:16-17; Daniel 9:18-19]

1. Father Lord, thank you because you are a prayer answering God, in Jesus' name.

2. Let the troublers of my life hear the voice of my prayers, in Jesus' name.

3. Every enemy of my prayer life; be frustrated, in Jesus' name.

4. O Lord, hear me when I cry, in Jesus' name.

5. Let my tears attract divine attention, in Jesus' name.

6. Let my prayers open heaven for immediate answers, in Jesus' name.

7. God of mercy, release your angels to minister on my behalf, in Jesus' name.

8. Let my prayers magnetize manifold mercies of God, in Jesus' name.

9. Let my prayers bring salvation and deliverances, in Jesus' name.

10. By my prayer O God, save me from every enemy, in Jesus' name.

11. Let the answers to my prayers terminate the evils of my life, in Jesus' name.

12. O Lord, by your power; take me away from the camp of my enemies, in Jesus' name.

13. Any problem dominating my life, hear the voice of my prayers and end, in Jesus' name.

14. Let my prayers bring down righteousness, in Jesus' name.

15. Mercy of God, take my prayers to the Almighty for answers, in Jesus' name.

16. Let my prayers bring down God's power and glory, in Jesus name.

17. Mercy of God, empower my prayer to attract good things, in Jesus' name.

Day 6

MERCY OF GOD, REMEMBER ME

[Psalms 25:7; 136:23; Jeremiah 31:20]

1. Mercy of God, remind my helpers to help me, in Jesus' name.

2. Mercy of God, advertise my handwork, in Jesus' name.

3. Mercy of God, command blessings into my life, in Jesus' name.

4. Mercy of God, destroy the root of sin in my life, in Jesus' name.

5. Let the sins of my youth be wasted by divine mercy, in Jesus' name.

6. Let the goodness of God clear me from every guilt, in Jesus' name.

7. Every dark room in my life; receive divine mercy, in Jesus' name.

8. O Lord, arise and command prosperity into my life, in Jesus' name.

9. Mercy of God, cause heaven to remember me for good, in Jesus name.

10. Father Lord, by your mercy; take me to the next level, in Jesus' name.

11. Every satanic limitation in my life, disappear by divine mercy, in Jesus' name.

12. Lord Jesus, take me from low estate to high estate, in Jesus' name.

13. Every evil power hiding my greatness; release it by force, in Jesus' name.

14. Blood of Jesus, mingled with divine mercy; advertise my greatness, in Jesus' name.

15. O Lord, by your mercy, make my life pleasant everywhere, in Jesus' name.

16. Mercy of God, remember me and advance my personality, in Jesus' name.

17. O Lord, for sure, have mercy upon me, in Jesus' name.

MERCY OF GOD, SEE ME THROUGH

[Psalms 69:16-17; 31:16; 67:1; Isaiah 54:7-8]

1. O God of mercy, open great doors for me by fire, in Jesus' name.

2. Let the forces of heaven command mercy into my life, in Jesus' name.

3. Every flood of problem in my life; die by divine mercy, in Jesus' name.

4. Every enemy of my breakthrough; die by divine mercy, in Jesus' name.

5. Every hindrance on my way; clear by divine mercy, in Jesus' name.

6. Every arrow of problems in my life; backfire by divine mercy, in Jesus' name.

7. Every mountain on my way to success; disappear by divine mercy, in Jesus' name.

8. Every reproach in my life; die by divine mercy, in Jesus' name.

9. Every yoke of suffering and hardship in my life; break, in Jesus' name.

10. By divine mercy, I jump over the fence of bondage, in Jesus' name.

11. Every weapon of the enemy in my life; become blunt by divine mercy, in Jesus' name.

12. By the mercies of God, let His face shine upon me, in Jesus' name.

13. Mercy of God, take me away from where I am to where you want me to be, in Jesus' name.

14. Let the mercies of God take me away from darkness to divine light, in Jesus' name.

15. Every wicked plan against my life; be destroyed by divine mercy, in Jesus' name.

16. Mercy of God, expose me to people that matter in the society of Christ, in Jesus' name.

17. Let my name ring a bell in the ears of great people on earth, in Jesus' name.

18. Let heaven begin to celebrate my ministry by divine mercy, in Jesus' name.

Thank You!

Beloved, I hope you enjoyed this book as much as I believe God has touched your heart today. I cannot thank you enough for your continued support for this prayer ministry.

I appreciate you so much for spending time to read this book and if you have an extra second, I would love you to leave a short review for this book on Amazon. There's no greater way to thank me than this! CLICK HERE TO LEAVE A REVIEW

Think of it as a testimony to other believers about how this book helped you and could benefit them. You can help me help others.

If you loved it then please let me know that too!

Thank you again, and I wish you nothing less than success in life.

God bless you.

Other Books by Prayer Madueke

1. 100 Days Prayers to Wake Up Your Lazarus

2. 15 Deliverance Steps to Everlasting Life

3. 21/40 Nights of Decrees and Your Enemies Will Surrender

4. 35 Deliverance Steps to Everlasting Rest

5. 35 Special Dangerous Decrees

6. 40 Prayer Giants

7. Alone with God

8. Americans, May I Have Your Attention Please

9. Avoid Academic Defeats

10. Because You Are Living Abroad

11. Biafra of My Dream

12. Breaking Evil Yokes

13. Call to Renew Covenant

14. Command the Morning, Day and Night

15. Community Liberation and Solemn Assembly

16. Comprehensive Deliverance

17. Confront and Conquer Your Enemy

18. Contemporary Politicians' Prayers for Nation Building

19. Crossing the Hurdles

20. Dangerous Decrees to Destroy Your Destroyers (Series)

21. Dealing with Institutional Altars

22. Deliverance by Alpha and Omega

23. Deliverance from Academic Defeats

24. Deliverance from Compromise

25. Deliverance from Lukewarmness

26. Deliverance from The Devil and His Agents

27. Deliverance from The Spirit of Jezebel

28. Deliverance Letters 1

29. Deliverance Letters 2

30.   Deliverance Through Warning in Advance

31.   Evil Summon

32.   Foundation Exposed (Part 1)

33.   Foundations Exposed (Part 2)

34.   Healing Covenant

35.   International Women's Prayer Network

36.   Leviathan The Beast

37.   Ministers Empowerment Prayer Network

38.   More Kingdoms to Conquer

39.   Organized Student in a Disorganized School

40.   Pray for a New Nigeria

41.   Pray for Jamaica

42.   Pray for Trump, America, Israel and Yourself

43.   Pray for Your Country

44.   Pray for Your Pastor and Yourself

45.   Prayer Campaign for a Better Ghana

46.   Prayer Campaign for a Better Kenya

47. Prayer Campaign for Nigeria

48. Prayer Campaign for Uganda

49. Prayer Retreat

50. Prayers Against Premature Death

51. Prayers Against Satanic Oppression

52. Prayers for a Happy Married Life

53. Prayers for a Job Interview

54. Prayers for a Successful Career

55. Prayers for Academic Success

56. Prayers for an Excellent Job

57. Prayers for Breakthrough in Your Business

58. Prayers for Children and Youths

59. Prayers for Christmas

60. Prayers for College and University Students

61. Prayers for Conception and Power to Retain

62. Prayers for Deliverance

63. Prayers for Fertility in Your Marriage

64. Prayers for Financial Breakthrough

65. Prayers for Good Health

66. Prayers for Marriage and Family

67. Prayers for Marriages in Distress

68. Prayers for Mercy

69. Prayers for Nation Building

70. Prayers for Newly Married Couple

71. Prayers for Overcoming Attitude Problem

72. Prayers for Political Excellence and Veteran Politicians (Prayers for Nation Building Book 2)

73. Prayers for Pregnant Women

74. Prayers for Restoration of Peace in Marriage

75. Prayers for Sound Sleep and Rest

76. Prayers for Success in Examination

77. Prayers for Widows and Orphans

78. Prayers for Your Children's Deliverance

79. Prayers to Buy a Home and Settle Down

80. Prayers to Conceive and Bear Children

81. Prayers to Deliver Your Child Safely

82. Prayers to End a Prolonged Pregnancy

83. Prayers to Enjoy Your Wealth and Riches

84. Prayers to Experience Love in Your Marriage

85. Prayers to Get Married Happily

86. Prayers to Heal Broken Relationship

87. Prayers to Keep Your Marriage Out of Trouble

88. Prayers to Live an Excellent Life

89. Prayers to Live and End Your Life Well

90. Prayers to Marry Without Delay

91. Prayers to Overcome an Evil Habit

92. Prayers to Overcome Attitude Problems

93. Prayers to Overcome Miscarriage

94. Prayers to Pray During Honeymoon

95. Prayers to Preserve Your Marriage

96. Prayers to Prevent Separation of Couples

97.   Prayers to Progress in Your Career

98.   Prayers to Raise Godly Children

99.   Prayers to Receive Financial Miracle

100. Prayers to Retain Your Pregnancy

101. Prayers to Triumph Over Divorce

102. Queen of Heaven: Wife of Satan

103. School for Children Teachers

104. School for Church Workers

105. School for Women of Purpose: Women

106. School for Youths and Students

107. School of Deliverance with Eternity in View

108. School of Ministry for Ministers in Ministry

109. School of Prayer

110. Speaking Things into Existence (Series)

111. Special Prayers in His Presence

112. Tears in Prison: Prisoners of Hope

113. The First Deliverance

114. The Operation of the Woman That Sit Upon Many Waters

115. The Philosophy of Deliverance

116. The Reality of Spirit Marriage

117. The Sword of New Testament Deliverance

118. Two Prosperities

119. Upon All These Prayers

120. Veteran Politicians' Prayers for Nation Building

121. Welcome to Campus

122. When Evil Altars Are Multiplied

123. When I Grow Up Visions

124. You Are a Man's Wife

125. Your Dream Directory

126. Youths, May I Have Your Attention Please?

Free Book Gift

Just to say Thank You for getting my book: Prayers For

Mercy, I'll like to give you these books for free:

Click here to download these books now

If you're reading this from the paperback version, email me at prayermadu@yahoo.com.

Your testimonies will abound. Click here to see my other books. They have produced many testimonies and I want your testimony to be one too.

An Invitation to Become a Ministry Partner

In response to several calls from readers of my books on how to partner with this ministry, we are grateful to provide our ministry's bank details.

Be assured that our continued prayers for you will be answered according to God's word. And as you remain faithful by sowing seeds of faith, God will never forget your labours of love in Christ.

Send your Seed to:

In Nigeria & Africa
Bank Name: Access Bank
Account Name: Prayer Emancipation Missions
Account Number: 0692638220

In the United States & the rest of the World
Bank Name: Bank of America
Account Name: Roseline C Madueke
Account Number: 483079070578
Routing Number (RTN): 021000322

Visit the donation page on my website to donate online: www.madueke.com/donate.

Printed in Great Britain
by Amazon

47868949R00177